WHY WE QUILT

WHY WE QUILT

CONTEMPORARY MAKERS SPEAK OUT

The Power of Art, Activism, Community, and Creativity

THOMAS KNAUER

Storey Publishing

The mission of Storey Publishing is to serve our customers by
publishing practical information that encourages
personal independence in harmony with the environment.

EDITED BY Deborah Balmuth and Michal Lumsden

ART DIRECTION AND BOOK DESIGN BY Carolyn Eckert

TEXT PRODUCTION BY Jennifer Jepson Smith

INDEXED BY Nancy D. Wood

COVER PHOTOGRAPHY, including front and back inside by
Mars Vilaubi, except © Chawne Kimber, back (top center);
© Denyse Schmidt, spine (top)

INTERIOR PHOTOGRAPHY BY Mars Vilaubi

ADDITIONAL PHOTOGRAPHY BY © Alan Radom, 98 (from the
collection of Trissa Hill), 101, 164; Alethea Morrison, 212 author; courtesy
of Allison Dutton, 37 t.l., 48; © Amy Friend, During Quiet Time LLC,
37 t.r., 54, 55; © Anne Sullivan, 37 b.l., 82; Courtesy of Brigitte Heitland,
177; © Brooklyn Museum of Art, New York, USA. Gift of Alice Bauer
Frankenberg/Bridgeman Images, 13 l.; © Carol Gander, 15; © Chawne
Kimber, 136, 150–154, 208 l.; © Cheryl Brickey, quilted by Cheryl
Brickey using Christa Watson's pattern "Rain" from *Machine Quilting with
Style* (Martingale, 2015), 56–57; © C&T Publishing, 94, 97 (from the
collection of the International Quilt Study Center & Museum, University
of Nebraska-Lincoln, 2016.009.0004); © Denyse Schmidt, iv l., 22–28;
© Diane Pedersen of C&T Publishing, Inc., 88, 91; © Earamichia Brown,
30, 33; © Eric Lubrick Photography, iv c.l., 149; © F+W Media, Inc., iv
c.r., 72, 184, 189; Courtesy of F+W Media, Inc., 168; © Gregory Case,
129; © Hearts & Hands Media Arts from the film *Hearts & Hands, 19th
Century Women and Their Quilts*, 44; Courtesy of Heather Jones, 134–135;
© Heidi Parkes, 37 b.r., 47; © Henrik Kam, v c.r., 58, 61; © Hisham
Ibrahim/PhotoV/Alamy Stock Photo, 3

ADDITIONAL PHOTOGRAPHY CREDITS ON PAGE 211

QUILT PATTERNS BY THE AUTHOR

TEXT © 2019 BY THOMAS KNAUER

Storey Publishing
210 MASS MoCA Way
North Adams, MA 01247
storey.com

Printed in China by R. R. Donnelley
10 9 8 7 6 5 4 3 2 1

Library of Congress Cataloging-in-Publication Data on file

Storey books are available at special discounts when purchased in bulk for premiums and sales promotions as well as for fund-raising or educational use.
Special editions or book excerpts can also be created to specification. For details, please call 800-827-8673, or send an email to sales@storey.com.

FOR ALL THE
QUILTERS OUT THERE
MAKING THEIR
OWN PRIVATE HISTORIES.

FOR SIMON, MATILDA,
AND KATHERINE.
THEY KNOW WHY.

CONTENTS

Why I Quilt

MY FAMILY CAME FROM LANCASTER, PENNSYLVANIA — home to the nation's largest community of Amish, who are famously iconic quilters — but I didn't grow up with quilts. My mother and grandmother were knitters, so we slept under store-bought comforters and the occasional knit afghan.

I suppose I first really became aware of quilts when, as a college student, I encountered the AIDS Memorial Quilt. The concepts of quilts as activism, quilts as memorials, and quilts as voices all appealed to me profoundly. And yet, though I found the AIDS quilt inspiring, I never thought about picking up needle and thread and *making* a quilt.

It wasn't until my daughter was born that I truly embraced my first quilt. A friend's mother sent baby Bee a wonderful baby quilt, and of course our first question was, "How do we take care of it?" The answer, "Wash it when it gets dirty," has stuck with me through my years of quilting. I make quilts that are meant to be used, even as they are social commentary. And yes, some of them have stains that just won't come out.

But I am getting ahead of myself. When my daughter was a toddler, I got a contract to design quilting fabric. Making a quilt seemed like a logical exercise for me, something to do once to see how fabric works when cut up into small pieces. So I set about designing my first quilt. I then sat down at the sewing machine my mother-in-law had given us and made a quilt top. I threw everything at it: piecing, appliqué, even some bits of hand embroidery. I didn't have a clue what I was doing, which was probably for the best; I was working unconstrained.

Tea and Skittles, Thomas Knauer, 2015, 40 × 48"
By turning the shooting target that was sold after the killing of Trayvon Martin into a baby quilt and quilting it with text from the boy's obituary, I use this quilt to question a society that claims to protect children even as it sees children of color as threats, and even targets.

I finished that first quilt top in a couple of days and assumed it would be the only quilt I'd ever make. But then I showed it to my 2½-year-old daughter. She looked at it and her eyes grew wide. She asked, "Is that for me?" hoping beyond hope that it would be. When I said "Yes" she simply ran at me — and the quilt — and barreled into me. My arms folded around her, wrapping her in the quilt. She stood there in my embrace for a solid 30 seconds. This may not seem like much, but it was the first time since she was born she had really let me hug her. You see, my daughter is on the autism spectrum and, especially when she was so young, hugs registered to her as frightening restraint. But there, wrapped in that quilt top, for some reason she felt safe. If that one quilt top could have that effect, I immediately imagined what a house full of quilts might be like. And I set to making more and more quilts.

Then came the hard part: actually learning to quilt. Over the next year I probably made another 30 to 40 quilts, just trying out new techniques and practicing the ones I already knew. I essentially apprenticed myself to myself with the help of online tutorials and YouTube videos. At the same time, I dove into the history of quilting. I wanted to understand what came before and immerse myself in the tradition. I learned how to quilt on the fly, as I was making samples for the fabric I was designing, and as I made more and more quilts for Bee. It was only after that year of learning that I decided I was ready to start making some serious quilts.

As I started taking a run at being a professional quilter, I had to think deeply about what quilts meant to me and what I thought these objects were all about. To me quilts are a wonderfully loaded form; they come with so much history and so many associations stitched right into them. We associate quilts with bringing comfort — both physically and emotionally. We think of quilts as safe places to be. When we think of quilts, we cannot avoid the connection between the maker and the recipient; quilts connect us across time and space.

Self-Portrait with Illness: Disorder, Thomas Knauer, 2016, 80 × 60"
In skewing the parallel and perpendicular lines of traditional quilts, this quilt portrays medical disorders not as chaos but as an atypical organization of ordinary parts, the disorienting and at times debilitating reality of experiencing everything as slightly off.

All that is the backdrop for my quilting practice. So many of the quilts I make are resolutely uncomfortable. They deal with gun violence and rape, economic inequality and racial discrimination. But these quilts only work because they are antithetical to so much of what we generally think of when we think of quilts. My quilts are still materially comfortable, but they are emotionally fraught; they are in conflict with themselves.

Now that I have begun making these quilts I cannot imagine not making them. By juxtaposing the expectation for a quilt with the uncomfortable reality I portray, I can elicit sorrow and grief, anger and frustration: a whole range of emotions and responses I don't think would be possible in another medium. I make these quilts because these are the emotions I feel when I look out at the world around me. My goal is to distill those emotions into singular quilts that will hopefully move those who see them. I make these quilts because I am angry and need somewhere to put that anger. I make these quilts to reflect the world as it really is. Ultimately, I think of my quilts as archiving the things that should never be forgotten.

In the end, what draws me to quilts — and indeed what I think makes them relevant in the twenty-first century — is the sense that quilts are an archaic item that's no longer materially necessary. Today quilting is neither an expected practice nor a basic practicality; it is a conspicuous choice. Quilts are not about material need but instead fulfill other needs, personal needs that are unique to each quilter. For me, quilts offer a vehicle for protest, a means for venting my outrage. For others, they offer a step away from the same world my quilts comment upon. Either way, I think quilts remain relevant, and will continue to do so, precisely because we do not *need* them but rather want them. As long as we desire these things called quilts, they will resonate and live on.

One Child Is One Too Many, Thomas Knauer, 2017, 38 × 38"

Each year hundreds of children in the United States die in gun incidents and gun accidents (negligent homicides), whether as bystanders to a violent crime, by being in the wrong place when a gun is accidentally fired, or through gaining access to an unsecured gun. A variation of the traditional sunbonnet Sue pattern (see page 80), this quilt is my protest against the pervasiveness of a gun culture that allows these deaths to occur and does nothing to prevent them.

INTRODUCTION

THROUGHOUT THE PAST TWO AND A HALF CENTURIES OF AMERICAN QUILTING, ONE THING HAS REMAINED CONSISTENT: THE NEED TO CREATE. Yes, quilting was spurred on by the westward migration in the nineteenth century, when shelter was frequently provisional and the cold of winter was never far off. But quilting equally grew out of the parlors and sitting rooms of America's cities. The American quilting lexicon is an outgrowth of simple quilts and ornate appliqué, of four-patches and nine-patches as well as intricate needlework. It is the child of both practicality and expressive innovation. To understand why we quilt, and why quilts still hold such a special cultural position in today's convenience-driven world of disposable goods, we have to look beyond any singular motivation or unifying narrative; the history of quilting is one of countless stories and untold hours with needle, thread, and cloth.

Quilts, however, are never merely fabric and thread, seams and stitches; they are the product of a creative spirit. While the material conditions surrounding quilting have changed continually — from the availability of inexpensive cloth to the advent of sewing machines, from the rotary cutter to computerized quilting — the impulse to *make* has remained a constant. Even as the practical need for quilts waned with the growth of commercially produced goods, quilting has survived, even thrived.

Somehow quilting continues to fill a unique need, existing in a space in between the practical and the decorative, between tradition and innovation, the individual and the communal. Indeed, quilting holds a special place in the American psyche the way few arts and crafts do, perhaps because quilts are wrapped up in so many of the nation's foundational stories. Quilts have connected families and generations, individuals and communities. Even today they offer a profound sense of connection: to the past, to one another, and to our own creative impulses. Quilting

---

Improv Half-Log Cabin, Heather Jones, 2014, 50 × 62"

We no longer need quilts to stay warm
or to survive harsh winters, but quilts may well
fill other, less material, needs.

continues to resonate now, at the intersection of history and our current moment, by filling new creative needs and providing ever more novel means for self-expression.

From a utilitarian point of view, the fact that we still make quilts makes very little sense. Simply consider the process and all of the labor that goes into a single quilt: the cutting of large pieces of cloth into smaller pieces of cloth to be sewn back together again to form a larger piece of cloth. Yet even in the twenty-first century, as bedding is available in nearly infinite varieties, frequently costing far less that it costs to make a quilt, the practice of quilting flourishes.

Thus begins our discussion of why we quilt: we do *not* quilt out of material necessity. While some may question whether material need ever truly drove quilting, it is undeniable that today quilting is something other than a merely practical art. We no longer need quilts to stay warm or to survive harsh winters, but quilts may well fill other, less material, needs. Each of us has our own stories to tell through our quilts, and if we really listen, no two stories will be the same. Certainly, there are common themes surrounding the question of why we quilt, but those can be only the broad strokes. The real story of quilting lies in our individual practices: the quilts we share, the stories behind them, and the lives those quilts become a part of.

In this book I explore the nature of quilts, looking beneath the surface of the quilts we make in order to understand why we still make them. The chapters that follow present various contemporary and historical approaches to the making of quilts, from which you, hopefully, will glean some meaningful reasons for quilting's continued popularity. Ultimately, this book is an effort to make explicit what so many of us intuitively know: there is quite clearly something special about quilts that draws us to the practice. This book is my attempt to explain why we quilt.

The AIDS quilt remains to this day one of the most remarkable quilts, though it is perhaps more important as a document of the human condition. It records both grief and hope, is a memorial and a protest. These individual quilts, when they come together, encompass so many lives and, amazingly, exist on both monumental and intimate scales.

CHAPTER 1

WE QUILT TO CONNECT WITH A RICH TRADITION.

There is something magical
about being part of a practice that traces back
through the centuries.

The popular mythology of quilting suggests that frugality and necessity forced the practice, but the fuller picture of quilting history is both far richer and more complicated. It is a story of blending cultures and traditions, a narrative full of creative and technological leaps that transformed quilting from a practice accessible only to the wealthy into one of the most popular activities in the country. It is the story of innovation and the creativity of quilters across the country.

Therein lies some of the mystique of quilts: the labor of making a quilt has, at its core, changed very little over the centuries. Yes, we have sophisticated sewing machines now, but the ways in which we join fabric with thread have been essentially the same for hundreds of years. In taking up the practice, we join with the tradition and add our own voices to the story of quilting.

Some of us learned to quilt from a parent or a grandparent, so the connection we feel to the tradition is immediate and intimate: a familial attachment traced back through the medium of quilts. Each new quilt carries with it the history of those lessons, the time spent together, and the wisdom of those who taught us.

The labor of making a quilt
has, at its core, changed very
little over the centuries.

Others of us came to quilting on our own, motivated by one thing or another. Here the connection is more abstract: an imagined relationship to the quilters who came before us. Though I learned much of what I know from YouTube tutorials, I can nevertheless imagine myself sitting companionably with my great-grandmother, working on our quilts, joined together through the common language of the quilting tradition.

But this connection to the past can only explain so much. I believe there are other connections that we are seeking. So many of us lead fractured, frenetic lives, racing from one obligation to another. While this lifestyle can fill us with a sense of accomplishment, it leaves little time for community, for simply being together with others. Within this context I find the emergence of new quilt guilds all over the country, and the world, to be incredible. Guilds run counter to the urgency that seems to permeate our lives; they ask us to pause and take time to be together, to share what we make, to be a community of quilters.

At its core, quilting is more often than not a solitary activity; we work away by ourselves in our often-makeshift studios. Though the quilts we create serve to make connections

> Guilds . . . ask us to pause and
> take time to be together, to share what we make,
> to be a community of quilters.

between people, the practice of quilting can leave us feeling isolated. Guilds remind us that we are not alone in our practice, that we are not mad to spend our time sewing together small bits of fabric.

Furthermore, the quilts we make when we are alone are never discrete, isolated objects. They are part of a living tradition, one that is perpetually evolving. But its evolution is not just a matter of the trends and tendencies of different eras; the evolution of the quilting tradition is born of all of the individual quilts that we make. By participating in the practice of quilting, we ensure that quilting remains vital, for there would be no tradition, no practice of quilting, without its countless individual practitioners. By preserving the tradition of quilting, we perpetually make it new, adding to the meaning of quilts and the quilting community as we understand them.

Quilters take up the craft of quilting for myriad reasons, but so often it is the community of a guild that keeps us quilting. There we find a support system for our individual practices. There we receive encouragement and advice, empathy and understanding. There we are stitched into quilting's rich and enduring traditions.

THE ROOTS OF AMERICAN QUILTING

 In order to truly understand why we quilt today, why the practice still resonates so deeply in the American psyche, we need to look backward, to the roots and branches of the tradition. There we discover why our forebears were drawn to quilting and why such a diverse repertoire of quilting emerged within the American tradition.

The practice of quilting started long before the concept of an American experience even existed. By the early eighteenth century, though, settlement along the east coast of North America nurtured and transformed the quilting tradition. The earliest quilts we see in the colonies were imports, brought in from India via England (see opposite). The highly decorative *palampores* and chintz cloth from India were prized in colonial America but remained accessible only to wealthy colonists, who sought them for a variety of purposes. These impressive fabrics also made their way to Europe and the colonies as ready-made quilts. In England,

and eventually in the colonies, these Indian imports blended with Western needlework and quilting traditions, creating all new forms and practices.

These early quilts were primarily wholecloth, made either of a single, beautiful cloth or white cloth adorned by intricately appliquéd pieces, particularly through a process known as *broderie perse* (see page 10). In *broderie perse*, French for "Persian embroidery," individual motifs were cut out of chintz and appliquéd onto the backing cloth to produce a larger design from the diverse parts. These quilts largely followed the model of Indian *palampores*, with a central focal element surrounded by various decorative motifs. Here we can see the start of a distinct quilting practice: though Indian imports inspired these wholecloth quilts, a blending of sensibilities emerged. The resulting quilts were not simple imitations. Rather, they incorporated aspects of the neoclassicism of the late eighteenth century, frequently borrowing common Greek or Roman motifs such as urns full of flowers

An example of an early *palampore* imported to America. The elaborate printing of this fabric was highly prized in the American colonies. (Maker unknown, circa 1750–1770.)

or architectural details. In the process, a new quilting vocabulary evolved.

Over time the wholecloth approach gave way to a new vogue in quilting that retained some aspects of the earlier *broderie perse* quilts and expanded on them. These quilts kept the key feature of a central, primary design but confined that motif to a single central square that was then surrounded by multiple, highly decorative borders.

In the first decades of the nineteenth century, production of high-quality printed cotton cloth became increasingly mechanized, first in Europe and then in America. These industrial advances made it possible to produce a wider range of designs at a lower price. As a result, new expressive possibilities opened up.

TOP LEFT: This wholecloth quilt with *broderie perse* borrows a common theme from Indian *palampores*: the tree of life. But here the floral motifs are appliquéd onto the wholecloth background, integrating different pieces of fabric into a single design. (Maker unknown, circa 1780–1800.)

BOTTOM LEFT: This excellent example of *broderie perse* has different floral motifs worked in a concentric design. The ample white space lets the quilting come forward in its own visual language. (*Medallion*, maker unknown, circa 1820–1840.)

Fabric manufacturers — already thinking about quilters and their needs — specifically printed large motifs for the center square element of a quilt design, to be used as is or with *broderie perse*. At the same time, quilters really began flexing their creativity in the borders. Some borders used wide strips of cloth just as they were, while others involved ever more sophisticated and compelling border designs.

In a sort of hybrid style carried over from the wholecloth tradition, *broderie perse* borders were made of one or more motifs taken from the printed cloth. At the same time, unique appliqué designs with shapes independent of the cloth they were cut from began appearing as well, with all manner of flora being cut from small-print cloth (see right). Finally, we began to see pieced borders made of four-patches, flying geese, and other simple blocks (see pages 45 and 12, respectively).

All of these examples are still very much whole-quilt designs, which use a single cohesive design element rather than block-by-block construction, but they show how quilters were beginning to move beyond wholecloth. In this important creative shift, quilt designs were no longer merely applied to a background. Instead, they were built up and pieced together to create something larger and greater than the individual parts

This later example of a tree of life quilt shows the transition from appliquéd quilts to pieced quilts, with the tree motif integrated into a more complex overall design that includes borders of *broderie perse* and pieced borders. (*Tree of Life*, maker unknown, circa 1790–1810.)

(as seen above). This shift is extremely significant: as quilters began putting more and more of their creative energy into these borders, they were laying the groundwork for the emergence of fully pieced quilt tops.

These early years of American quilting prepared the way for the development of a truly American art form. As individual quilters put their own spin on the conventions of the day, new forms and practices expanded the realm of possibility for quilting. These early creative leaps set out a founding visual vocabulary, the impact of which we still feel today.

While this quilt's center medallion still employs appliqué, its pieced elements are the dominant visual details. With half-square triangles, flying geese, diamonds, and pinwheels, it is almost a sampler of early American piecing. (*Medallion*, maker unknown, circa 1820–1840.)

Early Design Concepts

A **whole-quilt** design is one with a single, pieced design that occupies the entire space of the quilt rather than a series or group of distinct blocks. Common whole-quilt designs are large star quilts such as the star of Bethlehem (see page 39).

Wholecloth quilts are made using a single piece of cloth rather than piecing together smaller pieces of cloth. The design of a wholecloth quilt may be executed entirely through the quilting stitched through the layers or may include appliqué elements.

The **flying geese** block is a common and versatile block in which a triangle is set into a rectangle. Flying geese blocks arose early in the American quilting tradition (see left).

Alexis Deise

I quilt to honor a traditional art form and to bring it relevance in the modern era. The history of quilting as an art practiced primarily by women is important to me. I work within the confines of quilting traditions, utilizing traditional techniques such as hand quilting and hand appliqué, as well as incorporating traditional patterns and designs. By merging these elements with contemporary color palettes and alternative compositions, I hope to create a link between past and present.

Bars, 2015, 48 × 48"

This is a wonderful take on a traditional bars quilt; what is usually geometrically clean
has been transformed here into a cacophony of stripes and variations. It is amazing how much
movement can be achieved with such a limited visual vocabulary.

Laura Hartrich

I love that quilts are a nearly universal symbol of comfort and warmth. I quilt because it means I get to spend time with the ladies, and a few men, in my local quilt guild. I love being tied through a shared craft to a group of people of all ages and backgrounds. I love feeling part of the tradition of quilting. For me, the act of quilting is imbued with hope.

I quilt because I love to work with my hands and my eyes. I love playing with color and pattern. I love making a thing from start to finish. I love that when I'm done with that thing, it can be an object of comfort and utility, or it can be art. In some cases it can be both, and I love that, too.

Quilt for Our Bed, 2015, 108 × 108"
This original design incorporates elements of the traditional drunkard's path quilt pattern.

Stephanie Zacharer Ruyle

I see each quilt as a chance for a new beginning with a rich collective past; I have license to do whatever I like, by whatever method I choose, and I freely mix garment-sewing techniques and fabrics in my quilts. Thanks to my quilting communities, both in my area and those that I have joined at a distance, I am part of a unique fabric of collective creativity that keeps me engaged and always looking for new ways to both challenge myself and engage others.

18

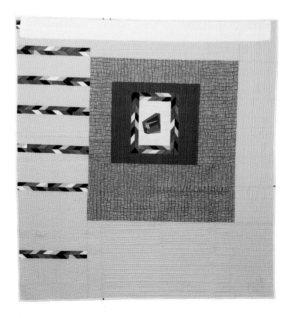

Read between the Lines, 2014, 57 × 54½"

OPPOSITE: quilt back. ABOVE: quilt top. This quilt is all about the delicate line work that moves over the piece.
It's as though the small blocks of red fabrics are invading the rest of the quilt. While the scale
of the line work is small, it is remarkable how much the lines capture both the eye and the imagination.

Debbie Grifka

It feels good that, in quilting, I am doing something women have done for generations. I understand the long line of women who loved sewing and took the opportunity to make something essential into something beautiful that reflected their own personalities, thoughts, and feelings about the world around them. I grew up without any extended family in my life, so working with fabric helps connect me to those I never knew. One of the most delightful things about making a quilt is that you put all your love into something that keeps people you care about warm.

Forever, 2015, 80 × 80"
Debbie's design for *Forever* was inspired by a beautiful ceiling and traditional quilt patterns such as orange peel and double wedding ring (see pages 29 and 76). Repeating the block design as the quilting design in some of the blocks helps to convey the impression of something worn over time, like the engraving on the inside of a wedding ring. The soft gold color extends the idea of the joy, comfort, and security of a long marriage.

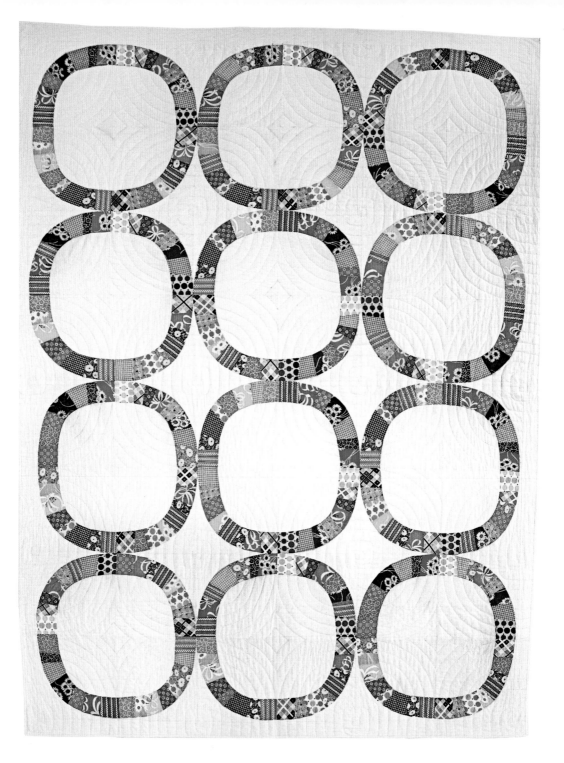

DENYSE SCHMIDT

In her quilting, Denyse Schmidt consistently plays back and forth between tradition and modernity with a remarkable subtlety. Her quilts blend improvisation and structure, producing work that offers a quiet yet commanding presence. I remember seeing her *Single Girl* quilt for the first time and marveling in the simple brilliance of that design. I have been a fan of Denyse's quilts ever since I started quilting.

The first quiltlike thing I remember is a cheater-cloth printed comforter. (See page 29.) It was machine-quilted and coordinated with a Sears chenille bedspread I had that created mountains of orange dust bunnies. I think the design was pseudocolonial, but I mostly remember the colors: harvest gold and burnt orange, an earthy brown palette. I was young, so it was probably in the mid-1970s.

Years later, when taking some art classes at the Worcester Art Museum school, I played around with a crazy-quilt aesthetic with fabric on paper. At the time I was working for a small clothing designer in his atelier. It would be another several years before I made my first quilts. They were gifts and pretty traditional in form.

Single Girl, 2007, 66 × 88"

This may be the most important quilt of the new century. It is a beautiful comment on the traditional double wedding ring quilt design, asserting that single life deserves a quilt of its own. Here the status of being single is something to be celebrated. For me, this will always stand as an extraordinary liberation quilt.

I fell in love with quilts that were like the scratchy, amateur fiddle tunes I loved: quilts that were made with joy for utility, at whatever skill level the maker had.

After I graduated from the Rhode Island School of Design, I moved to Connecticut to work in graphic design and be with my boyfriend at the time, who was a traditional boat builder and fiddler. I was feeling disconnected from friends and was increasingly dissatisfied with my graphic design career. I longed for a sense of community and felt a strong need to make tangible, lasting things with my hands, rather than ephemeral work produced on a computer.

Mainly because of the Appalachian fiddle music my boyfriend played, I turned to the nostalgia of barn raisings, old-fashioned quilting bees, and the colorful, eccentric quilts I discovered in books. I fell in love with quilts that were like the scratchy, amateur fiddle tunes I loved: quilts that were made with joy for utility, at whatever skill level the maker had, rather than quilts that were made to showcase fine skills.

Today I still like to make quilts that can feel timeless. I draw on traditional methods and use fabrics that might feel vaguely of another time, and I bring to the process all the influences of my culture and personal experiences, skills, and interests. I like this juxtaposition of then and now, of new and old. It might manifest in playing with the scale or placement of blocks, use of color, or focusing on the most simple and spare gesture.

Burlap & Horses, 2007, 86 × 93"

I am self-taught as a quilter, although I have been sewing since I learned from my mother when I was a girl. I took home economics classes in high school and worked in the costume shop at a theater during high school and college summers. In college I studied theater, and after college I picked up odd sewing-related jobs, mostly apparel-based. I'm sure I used some quilting books — including a Marianne Fons one, I think — when I made my first quilts, but I was always one of those who looked at the pictures and figured it out, wrong or right!

When I started my quilt business, my aim was to get people in my "tribe" — designers and artists — to see and love quilts the way I did. For many of my friends and acquaintances, the only quilts they knew were dark and dreary polyester things their aunt or grandmother had made for them that they may have appreciated but didn't want to live with. I wanted them to know that quilts weren't all perfect seams or "correct" color combinations. I wanted to show them quilts that were eccentric and full of personality.

In that light, quilts seem especially important in this age of digital and instant everything. They are tangible and useful, in contrast to so much in our lives that is temporary and virtual. Because the practical essence of a quilt is important to me, I always make quilts specifically for the bed, in bed sizes. Quilts take a certain amount of time and focus to create, and this is the best antidote to the speed at which we are inundated with information and changing ideas and perspectives.

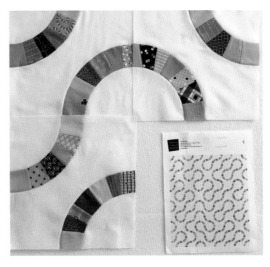

OPPOSITE: *Tangerine/Poppy*, 2004, 68 × 88". ABOVE: a work-in-progress in Denyse's studio.

For me, quilts mean so many things, and it's one of the reasons I love them. When I speak about my work, I show an old mind-mapping exercise I did when thinking about starting my quilt business. It shows all the things that happen around that place where we love, where we sleep and dream, are sick, die, and are born. Quilts are part of the equation. They keep us warm and comfort us. They remind us of loved ones and of important moments in our lives. In making a quilt, one brings together disparate bits and pieces from different times and places and creates a new whole that is useful and beautiful.

Compass, 2012, 86 × 93"

Appliqué Elements and Cloth Design

Orange peel quilts are known by the football-like shape of their appliqué elements.
Though they are most commonly configured as seen in the motif on the right, to create an overall
quilt design, the orange peel element has been used in any number of ways over the years.

Cheater-cloth is fabric printed to look like pieced patchwork.

EARAMICHIA "ENCYCLOPEDIA" BROWN

I love Earamichia "Encyclopedia" Brown's pictorial quilts, which capture something essential about the human experience. As they comment on the world around her, Earamichia's quilts are sensitive, exuberant, and direct. In her work Earamichia lays everything out on the surface, so to speak, and the quilts she creates never fail to amaze me.

I first learned to quilt when I was an assistant district attorney in New York and one of my colleagues' then girlfriend (now wife) had a dream of starting a quilting bee to discuss issues of the day. She got a group of women together and we agreed to learn to quilt. We all purchased *Quilting for Dummies*, plus fabric and supplies. We met monthly for about six months and worked through the exercises in the book while sipping and getting to know one another.

During the first two months, I designed a queen-size quilt, made templates, cut out my squares, and began hand-stitching the top. Then I began the process of hand quilting the quilt. I stitched blocks together while waiting in court for cases to be called and on the train ride from Brooklyn to the Bronx. Of course I ended up putting the quilt away,

---

She Blooms, 2016, 42 × 34"

Notice Earamichia's take on black women's hair, seen here as something glorious and beautiful — not as a problem to be solved. In addition, the way in which the woman is taking root in the ground wonderfully signifies strength, stability, and permanence. I keep coming back to this quilt, and each time I do, I find it remarkably rich.

In a world of the microwave, instant gratification, speedy production, and consumption, quilts . . . remind us that some things are worth waiting for.

but eventually found myself making place mats, coasters, and quilted bags. Eleven years later, after I had already made quilts for other people, I pulled out that first quilt, ripped out the hand-stitched quilting I had begun, and used pearl cotton to finish the quilt.

My interest in and connection to quilts have evolved over the years. In college, as a member of the National Council of Negro Women, we sold family reunion cookbooks that featured the quilts of Faith Ringgold. I had the pleasure of meeting her and seeing a couple of her pieces. Initially I wanted to learn about quilts because no one in my family made them. I was fascinated by old hand-me-down heirlooms and Ringgold's quilts. I wanted to learn a skill that had warmed families for generations.

As time went by and my quiltmaking skills evolved, quilts became another form of expression. Quilting was a way for me to take one thing and weave it into something better. I have always loved textiles and color, and quilts became a means of expressing that love. The more I created, the more quilting became a form of true artistic expression. Quilting is like a puzzle: you have a bunch of pieces that, when pieced together, form a stunning picture. Add in the element of stitches and you have an additional dimension for expression.

Today the quilts I make, whether realistic, mixed-media, or bed quilts, all come from my need to create. Many of the pieces I make result from images I see in my day and

nighttime dreams. Sometimes things I read or images I see form the concepts for my art quilts. With these quilts I don't think I purposefully set out to say anything. Instead, they are more of an expression of what I am feeling or seeing in that period of my life.

I believe quilts are integral to the twenty-first century. They remind us of the skills and artistic expressions of generations past. With the use of technology and the innovative techniques of today, we have a way and a means of continuing this rich tradition, while creating new works of art and heirloom pieces. There remains a joy in receiving something that was produced by hand and gifted to you. In a world of the microwave, instant gratification, speedy production, and consumption, quilts continue to remind us that some things are worth waiting for.

A Woman's Worth, 2017, 48 × 36"

WE QUILT
TO EXPLORE
AND
EXPRESS
OUR
CREATIVITY.

Every quilt, whether made from a pattern
or completely improvised, is an
exploration of our own creative spirit.

 When we select fabrics, choose threads, and imagine the quilting, we stretch ourselves, making choices that are unique to us. In doing so we step out of the realm of the mundane and enter into a creative space that nurtures us.

I believe there is no hierarchy of creativity, that the creative process is different for each individual and defies any comparison. Far too many quilters dismiss their own work as not as creative as someone else's, but that misses the point of the creative endeavor. What matters is taking time out of our ordinary routines to engage in the generative practice of making.

Indeed, I think we miss the fundamental creative aspect of quilts when we just look at the totality. Each of the small, subtle decisions that come up while making a quilt offers a meaningful opportunity to engage in the creative process. It is in these manifold choices that we give inflection to our creative voices. When looked at in this way, we can see every quilt as a singular expression of something within us, a reflection of our creative selves.

Because quilts are made up of a vast number of small decisions about fabric and thread, about shape, scale, and relationship, they cannot help but be the product of a certain

> In a world where individual voices so often seem small in relation to the enormity of our media output, quilts facilitate individual expression.

expressive spirit. But beyond being a creative outlet, quilting is often also a personal outlet, a means of speaking out. In this way, quilting has a remarkable capacity to lend itself to countless voices and a seemingly endless array of expression. In a world where individual voices so often seem small in relation to the enormity of our media output, quilts facilitate individual expression.

These expressions are often abstract, not necessarily communicating a particular message, but sharing a sensibility, a mood, a feeling. Our quilts tend to reflect our preferences, and our preferences are reflections of our unique identities. For example, each of us is drawn to certain colors and shapes, though we may not ever really understand why. Somehow they just resonate with us. As such, our use of color and form are simply two of the countless personal expressions that we stitch into the quilts we make.

Sometimes we intend these expressions to be shared and seen by others, but just as often we make our quilts for ourselves. These quilts serve as reminders to ourselves of who we are and surround us with objects that talk to us; they are more than mute materials. Each quilt is an unmistakable expression of a moment in time, a moment in the maker's life. As the years pass, these quilts remain evocative of that particular moment, enduring as remarkable monuments to our lives.

These four examples show how four quilters use blocks to create four very different designs and effects.
CLOCKWISE FROM TOP LEFT: Allison Dutton, page 49; Amy Friend, page 54; Heidi Parkes, page 46; and Anne Sullivan, page 83.

THE MATURATION OF QUILTING

From its earliest history, quilting has been more an outlet for expression than a practical necessity. In many societies with a rich quilting history, the majority of household labor has long been relegated to women, while men worked outside the home. Quilts became a means for these women to create needed blankets and other practical household objects while also enjoying an artistic outlet. Often, quilting also offered women the benefits of community.

Yet if one factors in not only the cost of the cloth but also the many hours of handwork involved, we can see that making quilts was highly impractical at a time when women, even wealthier women, had many demands pulling at their days. Quilting would have been more closely associated with other forms of decorative needlework than with the countless necessary tasks.

But as the number of American fabric manufacturers grew exponentially in the first half of the nineteenth century, printed cotton cloth in countless designs became readily available and newly inexpensive. This cheaper cloth opened up the doors of quilting experimentation, and soon quilting had taken hold across the country. The abundance of cloth readily available in all manner of styles — from the simplest to the most highly decorated prints — smoothed the way for an expanding range of quilting practices. It is in this period that we see the decline of *broderie perse*, with its elaborately cut out designs, and a transition to original designs, with quilters producing their own expressions rather than borrowing motifs from the printed cloth.

38

Quilts became a means for . . . women to create needed blankets and other practical household objects while also enjoying an artistic outlet.

In this striking example of a whole-quilt design, a single design element — the star of Bethlehem — rather than a series of blocks dominates the quilt. (*Star of Bethlehem*, Walker family, circa 1830–1850.)

This transition to piecing, with its
simpler set of technical skills . . . facilitated the shift to
quilting as a national phenomenon.

While the frequently large motifs used in wholecloth *broderie perse* quilts required ample working space — a luxury not available to the majority of people — piecing could readily be done in one's lap. The importance of cloth's ready availability cannot be underestimated; without it quilting would have remained an extravagance. But it is this transition to piecing, with its simpler set of technical skills, that truly facilitated the shift to quilting as a national phenomenon.

As piecing began to take hold, many of the earliest fully pieced quilts were still whole-quilt designs. Throughout the first half of the nineteenth century, a variety of large star designs emerged (see page 39), revealing the innovative potential in piecing, not to mention the extraordinary creativity that went into making these remarkable quilts.

At the same time a whole new visual vocabulary of appliqué was emerging. Whereas in previous decades, the whole-quilt style of *broderie perse* wholecloth quilts influenced the development of appliqué techniques, now a block-based quilt structure served as the foundation. The main difference lay in the relationship of the appliquéd piece to the rest of the quilt: *broderie perse* appliqué relied on the printed cloth to provide the motif that was then cut out and sewn onto

This album quilt is a good example of appliqué stepping away from *broderie perse*. Instead of cutting out existing *broderie perse* motifs from chintz, the quiltmaker created an original appliqué design by cutting out and stitching on motifs from many different fabrics. (*Album*, Elizabeth Ann Gorsuch, circa 1840–1850.)

the wholecloth, while appliqué of pieced blocks was often made of simple or plain fabrics that were cut out and stitched on to create an original design. Some quilts employed appliqué blocks set alternately with blocks of patterned cloth. Others, known as *album quilts* (see opposite), which had distinct appliqué motifs in each block that produced an "album" of designs, became all the rage. Another popular use of appliqué was a single motif repeated across the quilt top, forming patterns and secondary relationships among the elements (see right).

These appliqué quilts represent the final step in transitioning from whole-quilt designs (such as the Bethlehem and Ohio stars; see pages 39 and 45, respectively) to a practice that more closely resembles the kinds of fully elaborated pieced-block quilts we most often see today.

The earliest block-based quilts were relatively simple in structure, employing a few basic designs such as the one-patch, the four-patch, and the nine-patch blocks (see page 42). But that basic vocabulary included the possibility of nearly infinite variation. By solely controlling color placement and relationship, a vast array of effects could be achieved, all kinds of variations created from a common core. And by adding in the popular flying geese and half-square triangles

Taking into account both positive and negative space, this is a beautiful example of an appliqué quilt. Together, the blue appliqué and the shapes made between the appliqué elements create a truly rich design. (*Papercut Appliqué*, maker unknown, 1856.)

(see pages 13 and 45), the range of possible designs became nearly infinite. Quilters all over the country took full advantage of the potential in these fundamental forms, which led to what might be considered a golden age of quilting.

Over the course of the second and third quarters of the nineteenth century, a distinctly American form of quilting emerged, born of and reflecting the time and place.

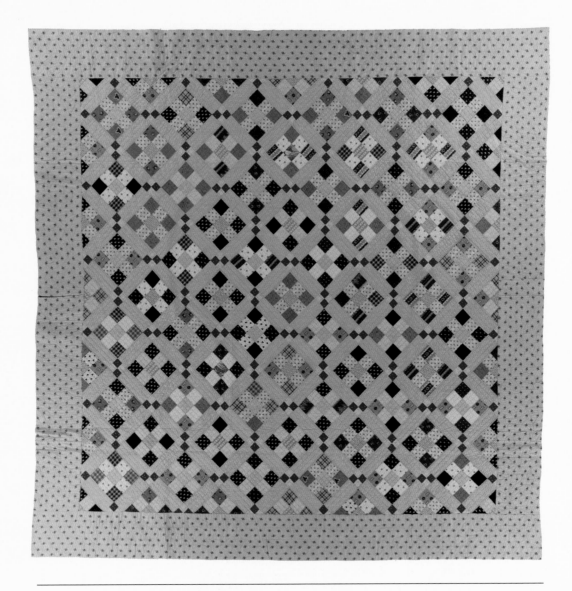

42

Here the traditional nine-patch blocks are turned on point, with the corners pointing up and down, to create a more dynamic space. As an extra detail the maker used four-patch blocks at the points where the yellow sashing intersects, adding another level of movement to the overall design.
(*Nine Patch*, Anna B. Eshleman, circa 1860–1870.)

> Over the course of a single century, quilts went from being a relative rarity to an absolute craze, an essential creative outlet for women of every class.

Starting in the 1860s with the mass production of the Singer sewing machine, quilts became more practical to make. But even so, more than ever quilters were making quilts for the sake of making quilts. We know that this expansion of quilting was not merely a matter of necessity — the need for warmth — because commercially produced blankets were widely and inexpensively available at the time. In addition, if necessity had been the force driving this quilting boom, it likely would have inclined quilters to make quilts in the fastest and easiest way possible. But that is not what we see.

The rise of block-based designs made quilting far more accessible. Now, basic sewing skills — like the ability to stitch a straight seam — were all one needed to make a quilt. While good stitches certainly mattered, the technique involved was far simpler than that of highly complicated appliqué. Importantly, the process had also become much faster. Over the course of a single century, quilts went from being a relative rarity to an absolute craze, an essential creative outlet for women of every class.

While the greater accessibility of materials and simpler stitching techniques were driving factors, I believe the most important reason for women across the United States

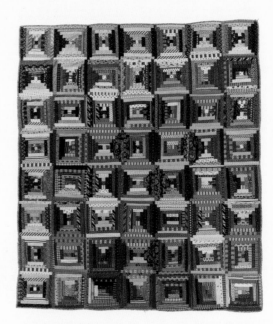

The log cabin quilt may well be the quintessential American quilt. This is a "courthouse steps" variation in which the stepped diamonds stand out. (*Log Cabin*, maker unknown, circa 1870–1890.)

This signature quilt was used to raise money for the Temperance movement. Signatories would have made a small donation in order to sign their name to one of the blocks. (*Crusade Quilt*, Ohio Woman's Christian Temperance Union members, 1876.)

the prevailing (male) culture. To be sure, quilting enabled creative self-expression, but it also brought women together in groups where their voices would be heard. In church and community sewing societies, women could exchange ideas and be themselves.

Women feeling increasingly constrained by notions of the feminine and the domestic also found a communal outlet at the fore-front of the century's reform movements. And they brought their quilts with them.

Quilts were used to raise funds for a wide range of activities, and they played an important role in supporting the Abolitionist, Temperance, and Suffrage movements (see page 140). Some quilts were made to be raffled or auctioned to support a cause. Others, known as *signature quilts* (see left), raised money by having signatories pay to have their names added to the quilt.

These quilts were ways for women to simultaneously support and speak out for the causes they believed in. Indeed, the very act of adding one's name to a signature quilt was a declaration, a public protest. The fact that quilts were so often used as a part of these movements illustrates just how essential quilting had become in American life.

taking up quilting was an overwhelming desire for creative expression. Quilting facil-itated creativity in an era when women were increasingly constrained and constricted by

Block-Based Designs

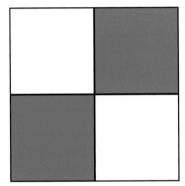 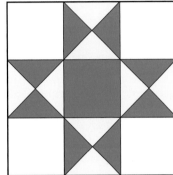 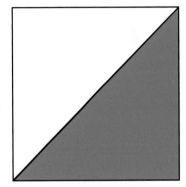

The **four-patch** block is made up of four squares, or patches, sewn together to make a larger square. Four-patch blocks can be set off individually or subsumed into a larger design scheme or pattern.

The **Ohio star** is an eight-pointed star design and is just one of quilting's many variations on the star motif.

The **half-square triangle** block is a square made up of two right-angle triangles sewn together. It is among the most common and versatile blocks in the quilting tradition.

Heidi Parkes

46

I quilt because hand sewing and fabric slow me down more than collage or painting, and that allows me to hear a subtler creative voice. I quilt because a 5' × 5' quilt can fold up into a carry-on or simple shipping box for exhibition, when a large painting couldn't even fit down my apartment staircase. I quilt because fabric, thread, and sewing needles are affordable, and because my studio is easily held within my living space. I quilt because each fabric has a source and a history that allow me to make art in a complex and collaborative world, rather than alone with a virgin white canvas. Mostly, I quilt because I have a lot to say about what a quilt can be; I believe that there is a great deal of unexplored potential in the medium, and it is one of the most exciting art forms today.

Places Unfold, 2014, 59 × 59"

The range of techniques used in this quilt yield such a rich variety of visual references. From maplike squares to others evocative of particular environments, this quilt offers us a sense of place through snippets of information. Perhaps it is not even a single space, but a journey taken, to which we are invited.

Allison Dutton

Though I've tried many creative endeavors over the years, quilting and sewing are the ones that have stuck the most. I love cutting fabric apart and creating something new, adding my own stitches to finish it, and (more often than not) gifting the finished quilt to someone who will love it and be comforted by it. I have a lot of fun trying out different techniques and patterns, and sometimes I make up my own. There are just so many quilts to make! I don't think I'll be stopping anytime soon.

49

Emerging Illusion, quilted by Allison Dutton (designed by Cheryl Brickey), 2015, 65 × 65"

Nydia Kehnle

I started quilting because I wanted my children to have something they could cuddle, something I could put my love into when creating it. But once I finished my first quilts, something shifted in me. I realized that I enjoyed the designing and puzzling of a new quilt, a new challenge with every project. It became my artistic outlet and my therapy.

50

Tessellation 3, quilted by Nydia Kehnle (designed by Nydia Kehnle and Alison Glass), 2014, 48 × 60"
Flat out, this is a spectacular quilt. Its use of shape and color evoke a sense of wild abandon.
While it is inevitably bound by its four sides, the quilt itself feels boundless in its scope and energy.

Jacey Gray

Although I learned sewing basics as a child (from my grandmother), it didn't take hold until I was in my twenties. I dabbled in garments and bags, and then I learned to quilt. It gradually became a (nearly) daily practice/obsession. Making patchwork is a creative outlet that helps me find balance. I love using scraps and mixing colors.

53

Strippy Strings, 2015, 57 × 69"

Amy Friend

I have studied and explored various media over the years, but when I left my job as a museum collections curator to stay home with my children, I found that I needed to do something that I could easily pick up and put down when my children woke up from their naps. It was at that time, in about 2009, that I discovered modern quilting online. Thanks to my mother and grandmother, I already had decent sewing skills, so I was able to teach myself to quilt using online tutorials. My quilts rarely have an intended use on a bed or are made to match a decor. I quilt to get a creative idea out of my head and into tangible form.

54

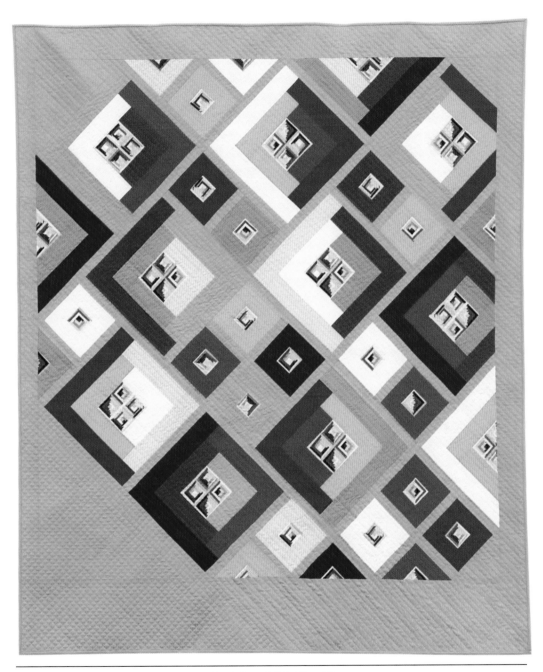

Possibilities, 2016, 55 × 65"

OPPOSITE: detail and back. ABOVE: quilt top. Both incorporate elements of the
traditional log cabin quilt pattern (see page 43).

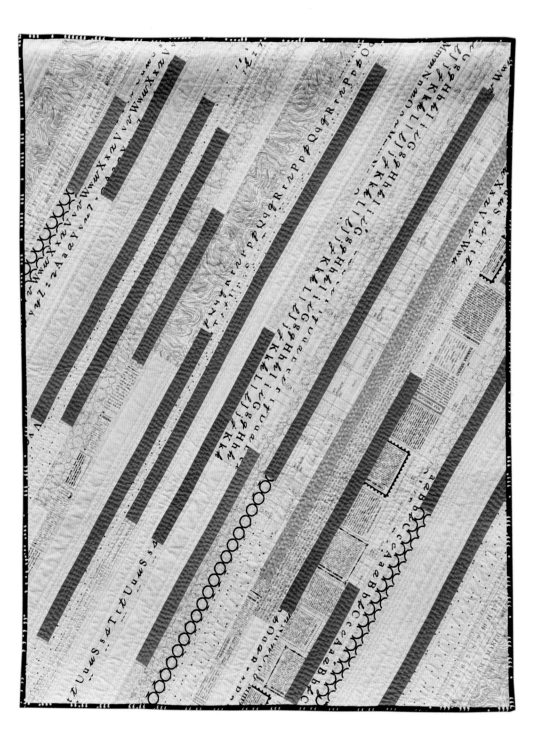

Cheryl Brickey

I quilt as a creative outlet. I love to take fabrics of all colors and prints and turn them into something that is not only beautiful but also useful. I enjoy seeing the quilt designs I have in my head come to life and being able to gift something handmade to a family member, friend, or even a stranger.

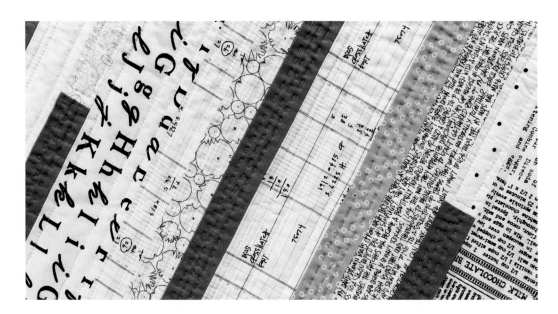

Drizzle, quilted by Cheryl Brickey (designed by Christa Watson), 2015, 40½ × 53½"
OPPOSITE: quilt top. This quilt is all about the fabric choices; the variety of text prints make the quilt feel like a deluge of language, a superabundance of script. At the same time, it is begging the viewer to get closer, to decipher the text or what seems a secret code. It is wonderful when design and fabric come together to make something that just feels so incredibly right. ABOVE: detail of *Drizzle*.

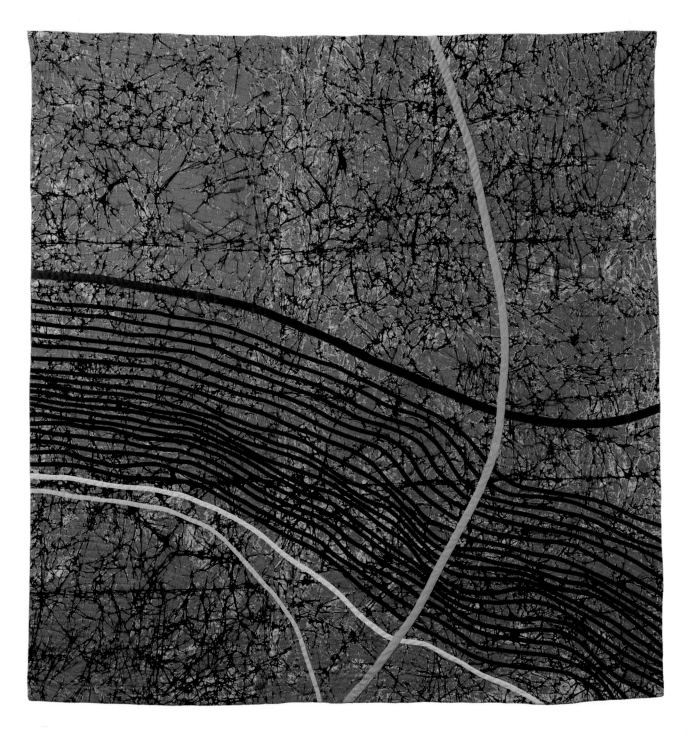

JOE CUNNINGHAM

Joe Cunningham's work rides a fine line between art and craft, embracing the best of both worlds to create a style that is uniquely his own. I first became aware of Joe's work when I was starting out as a quilter and have been a fan and a follower ever since. The aesthetic leaps that Joe makes in his quilts intrigue and amaze me, and I always look forward to his next creation.

■

My first quilt-related memory is helping my mother install fabric and batting in a borrowed quilt frame so she could tie comforters for us to use in the winter. It was not exactly a glorious quilt project, but I helped as she used a quilt frame, making it seem like a quilt was a part of normal life. I must have been around 8 or 9 years old. The making of my first quilt, though, is a far longer story.

Growing up outside of Flint, Michigan, on a dirt road, my main entertainment was books. My parents had an encyclopedia set that came with a set of Collier's Junior Classics, which were books of excerpts from classical literature for young people. From Beowulf to Swift to Cervantes, from *The Odyssey* to Grimm's fairy tales, poetry, fiction, and history, there was enough in those 10 books to give me an idea of culture far beyond anything I was getting at school. I continued to seek out books in libraries throughout my years growing up. Then, in a history class during eighth grade, we took a field trip to

Safety in Color, 2010, 72 × 72"

the Flint Institute of Arts. I walked into that hushed, artfully lit room of paintings and felt for the first time that I was home. This, I knew, was where I belonged.

My art teacher in high school told me I had no talent for art, but that didn't mean I could not appreciate it. I was playing guitar and drums in nightclubs by the time I was 15, so I had my art form. And I could go to the Detroit Institute of Arts as often as I could skip school. (The DIA is still a great museum!) From my teen years on I cultivated friendships with artists, always looking to learn more about the artistic life.

In 1979 a woman named Gwen Marston hired me to play guitar on some of her folk gigs, and one day I saw a box of antique quilts at her house. She had been awarded a grant to document the papers and quilt collection of Mary Schafer, who played an important role in the quilting revival of the 1970s. Marston had dozens of Schafer's quilts ready to be photographed. I had never heard quilts mentioned in connection with art, and yet here were these objects with an uncanny resemblance to art.

I had never heard quilts mentioned in connection with art, and yet here were these objects with an uncanny resemblance to art.

Island in Two Parts, 2010, 72 × 72"

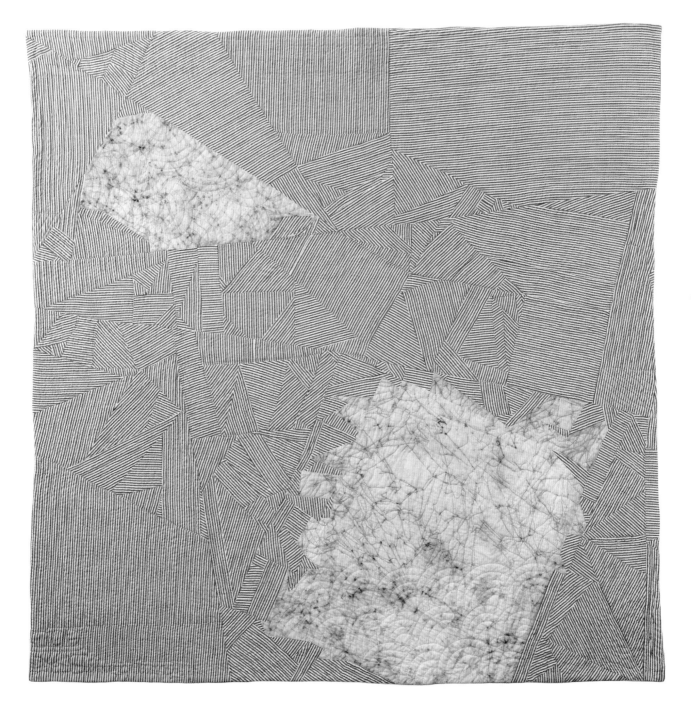

Marston said that gathering all the documentary information on the quilts was thrilling and fun, but confessed that she was dreading writing the catalog she was supposed to produce at the end of the project. When I offered to write the catalog for her, she said, "Well, you would have to learn about quilts." That was all I needed to hear. I started reading my way through the few books that were then available on the subject, from Marie Webster's 1915 *Quilts: Their Story and How to Make Them* right through the latest works by Jonathan Holstein and Patsy and Myron Orlofsky. When I met Schafer, it didn't take long for me to get the idea that she was one of the greatest quiltmakers alive.

One evening Marston knocked on my door. She brought me a small quilt top in a hoop, along with a thimble, needles, and thread. She explained that if I was going to write with authority about quiltmaking, I should know how to quilt. She showed me the rocking stitch she had learned from her Mennonite mentors and I finished the small piece in about a week.

Marston and I worked together for more than a decade. We traveled all over the country to teach quiltmaking and promote Schafer's work. Under Schafer's influence, Marston and I copied old quilts stitch for stitch, imitated many historical styles, and tried to work in ways that would let us get into the mind-sets of the old-time quiltmakers. Throughout the 1980s, we each began to find our own voices in quiltmaking.

Eventually, I realized that the quilts I was making had at least as much to do with the paintings I had studied as they did with the quilts upon which I had been so fixated. By 2000, it started becoming clear to me that what I had done was back myself into being an artist.

63

The Way Home, 2004, 74 × 74"

> What I am trying to do is make a
> functional quilted blanket that can both warm you
> against the coldness of the universe
> *and* look at home on the walls of any museum.

64

All my life I had believed that art was only for me to study and enjoy looking at. I never thought that maybe I could make art, too! By thinking of myself as a quiltmaker, never believing that I was making something so glorious and intimidating as Art, I was able to find my own artistic voice before I even realized I was seeking it.

The brilliance of American quiltmaking is that quilts can look like anything we can imagine. It is built into the DNA of the American quilt that we can sew anything together any way we want. What I am trying to do is make a functional quilted blanket that can both warm you against the coldness of the universe *and* look at home on the walls of any museum. Along the way, I am trying to show that a quilt can convey the entire realm of human experience, not only the pretty and nice part of our world. To make this kind of practical object that is also an object of art, one only has to walk through the door opened by American women of the nineteenth century into a realm of infinite creativity.

LYNETTE ANDERSON

I am drawn to Lynette Anderson's quilts because they so beautifully tell stories. Even if I am not privy to the entire story, it's clear that every detail contains meaning. Lynette's quilts are simultaneously personal and accessible, and she has a remarkable capacity for using images and materials to invite viewers (and makers) into her quilts. Hers is an exceptional voice in the quilting world, one that illustrates the global nature of quilting today.

I have always loved making things. Especially textile-related things, whether embroidered, knitted, painted, crocheted, hand-spun, or woven. I made my first quilt in 1981, after the birth of my first son, David. After making that quilt, I became hooked for life.

My first quilt was, of course, a sampler quilt (see page 71). At that time there were only a couple of quilt shops in the United Kingdom; my mum and I took a trip to London and I had my first visit to Liberty (an iconic department store), where I bought some amazing Tana Lawn fabrics. I hand-pieced and hand-quilted it and loved every moment. That quilt holds special memories for me of both the trip to buy the fabrics and the start of my journey to become a quiltmaker.

I believe all quilts tell powerful stories. Over the years, when I have seen an old quilt that spoke to me, I have, when possible, bought it and tried to glean as much historic information as I could about it. I am especially attracted to quilts that have embroidery.

Quilts that I have made tell different kinds of, and more personal, stories than the quilts I buy. In my early quiltmaking days I often used fabrics that were leftovers from dressmaking, rather than specific patchwork fabrics, and those quilts hold memories for me of who gave me the fabrics. Later, when I was still learning techniques, the quilt pattern was of particular interest.

Now my quilts start with my love of drawing, which I still do the traditional way, with pencil and eraser. Bringing the images that I have in my head to life on paper gives me so much pleasure. Then the fun begins, as I select fabrics and transfer my drawn concept into appliqués and simple piecing and add embroidery for texture and dimension. The mixing of fabric with embroidery is my all-time favorite look.

67

My quilts start with my love of drawing, which I still do the traditional way, with pencil and eraser.

OPPOSITE: *A Dog's Life*, 2011, 42 × 46"
ABOVE: transferring a drawing into pieced fabric.

In addition, creating buttons to add to my designs is an exciting process. First I draw, and then the drawings are made ready for "Lizzie" the laser machine. Watching Lizzie cut the little wooden shapes is mesmerizing. A team of local artists then hand-paints each button.

In these ways my quilts definitely tell stories. Each little picture that I create says something about an event in my life. It might be about something that happened to me this week or about something that happened over a period of years; either way, my quilts tell that story to you.

TOP LEFT: design wall.
BOTTOM: detail of *Chateau Hexagon*, 2013.

Anderson's Farm, 2016, 34 × 48"

Lynette's quilts quietly evoke a particular place: through the various panels
she offers us glimpses of moments, scenes in a life, that invite us to share in her own private world.
Her quilts leave no doubt that these are real places, lovingly shared with us. This original design incorporates
six traditional fox and geese blocks adjacent to the hearts in the center.

Creating the quilt I see in my mind's eye gives me a sense of satisfaction that is uplifting. Showing my creation — whether physically to a group of friends or by sharing a photo on social media — totally validates my creativity.

70

Scandinavian Christmas, 2009, 36 × 43"
In this quilt, Lynette works in several traditional churn dash quilt blocks bordering
the Christmas scenes in the center of the quilt.

Dabbling with Design Elements

A **sampler quilt** is made up of different block patterns that are all the same size but don't repeat.

CHAPTER
3

WE QUILT
TO MOVE
BEYOND
CONSUMER
CULTURE.

Quilts provide more than warmth;
they stand for an ethos of things, a belief that what
surround ourselves with matters and has meaning.

 Each quilt we make takes the place of commercially produced bedding, replacing the simple fact of a blanket's existence with multiple meaningful associations. As a handmade item, each quilt carries with it the labor and love of its maker. That love is then passed on to whomever uses that quilt.

In this light, quilts are subtle nudges toward a more intimate relationship with things and with our world. We live in an era of ubiquitous objects, of untold plenty right at our fingertips. In contrast to that, stitched into every quilt are countless hours of creative thought and intense work, and when we hold a quilt, we cannot help but see, feel, and appreciate the labor of another's hands. This pause to consider the nature of quilts is no small matter. Our quilts inevitably resensitize us to what lies beyond *things*. We begin to see not just what an object is, but also what it means. These lessons, once learned, never leave us; they ripple outward through our future selves.

The idea of rejecting mass-produced objects may partially explain why people continue to quilt and why quilting thrives in the face of modern alienation. What it doesn't tell us, though, is why people begin to quilt in the first place. Yes, some are actively looking for a connection to the past or are searching for a community, but I believe quilting is, in many ways, a logical reaction and response to the fast-paced world, full of disposable

elieve quilting is . . .
nd response to the fast-paced world,
able objects, in which we live.

t we

wing down to craft a quilt, we create a connection to the
ow a quilt is created makes quilting an intimate practice
because we must remain close to the materials we are working with.

74

Early in the twentieth century, German philosopher Walter Benjamin theorized that original objects give off a sort of aura that a reproduction lacks. In a similar way, I believe handmade items carry with them a similar emotional residue, a layer of meaning that cannot be found in a store-bought version. When looked at through this lens, quilting becomes a small and modern act of resistance, a rejection of a consumer culture in favor of something more personal.

It is easy to imagine a day when no one quilts anymore, a day when ease of access to commercially produced bedding and blankets renders quilting an anachronism. But that day has not yet come, despite ample potential. As quilters, every one of us is a preservationist, a partner in the enduring practice of quilting. Whether we know it or not, we are all activists standing against the passing of the tradition we love.

Detail of *Cooley Landing: Life in Water*, by Linda Gass. For more about Linda, see page 157.

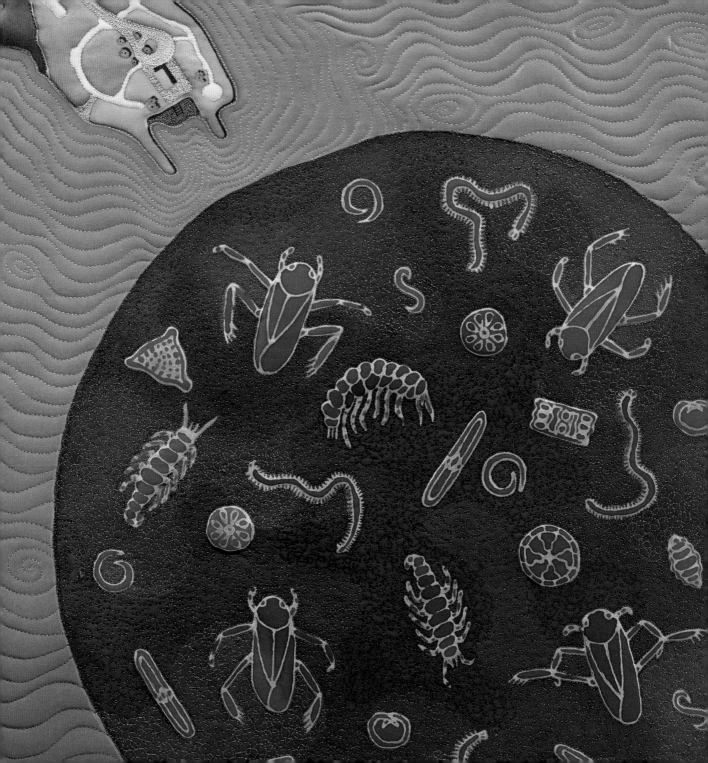

THE INTRODUCTION OF STANDARDIZATION

 As American cities boomed around the turn of the twentieth century, the popularity of quilting varied drastically according to geography. The practice fell out of favor for an urban population presented with more and more activities to occupy their leisure hours. At the same time, quilting thrived and remained extraordinarily vibrant in rural communities; quilters there were still taking the time to use needle and thread to make quilts.

The rural quilting community was so vibrant, in fact, that by the beginning of the twentieth century an entire industry had grown up to support it. Quilt kits became common; blocks and designs that had once been design innovations were drawn up and turned into printed patterns. The lexicon of quilting was becoming increasingly standardized. Some of the most iconic American quilt patterns — including the double wedding ring, the Dresden plate, and sunbonnet Sue (see opposite and page 80) — emerged during this period.

Quilting in this period was not disappearing, but it was changing. Although some inventiveness was being lost, the growing number of patterns made quilting accessible to women a generation or more removed from quilting's peak in the nineteenth century. In fact, the nascent quilting industry never would have developed if there wasn't a continued belief that quilting was a practice worth pursuing. It is during this period that national quilt exhibits and contests became popular. These new attractions further fueled a renewed interest in the quilting tradition.

This rise of patterns meant that more people were making the same quilt, but it also kept people quilting. Though quilt patterns began as a means to sell other products — most significantly magazines and batting — by the 1930s, stand-alone patterns and pattern books were widely available.

The double wedding ring, with its interlocking circles, or rings, is an iconic American quilt pattern that really took hold in the early twentieth century. (*Double Wedding Ring*, maker unknown, circa 1930–1940.)

77

> The need to make do with what was available fostered an intuitive creativity in quilters.

This quilt was likely made with feed sack cloth, reusing the muslin bags that contained flour and other dry goods to make something new. (*Star*, maker unknown, circa 1930–1940.)

It is remarkable that a quilting industry would take hold in the 1930s, during the height of the Depression. Yet quilting endured. Even as patterns and kits became more readily available, those who could no longer afford to purchase cloth specifically for quilts used any scraps they could find. Aware of this, companies began to make feed sacks of patterned muslin to be used in garments and quilts alike. Indeed, the need to make do with what was available fostered an intuitive creativity in quilters, who produced an impressive array of original scrap quilts (see opposite).

While the frugality of scrap quilts was essential to quilting's continuing prominence in the 1930s, it also sowed the seeds of decline. Following World War II, quilting — and the handmade in general — became increasingly associated with the poverty of the Depression. The 1950s ushered in the rise of modern consumer culture, in which shiny and new were the order of the day. Nowhere was this more evident than in America's suburbs.

Though the spread of the suburban ideal among the white population left little room for quilts, quilting remained remarkably vital among other populations. For rural America, the growing commodity culture seemed remote, and quilting continued to be an integral practice. It was here that much of the quilting tradition was (thankfully) preserved as urban and suburban America looked to the future.

This small quilt combines the traditional rail fence quilt pattern with a large piece of a feed sack label. The entire quilt was likely made with cloth recycled from feed sacks, as flour producers during the 1930s were making bags with patterned cloth. (*Rail Fence*, maker unknown.)

Iconic Patterns from the Early Twentieth Century

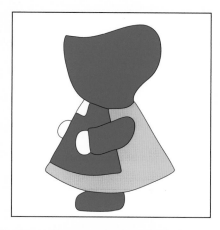

The **Dresden plate** is a quilt block containing a circular design composed of several individual blades, or wedges, that are sewn together to create a full circle. The ends of the blades may be squared off to create a neatly rounded circle or brought to a point to emphasize the individual blades.

Sunbonnet Sue is a traditional quilt block that was especially popular in the early twentieth century. It is made up of several pieces that, when appliquéd together, form the image of a little girl wearing a sunbonnet. For my twenty-first-century take on this pattern, see page x.

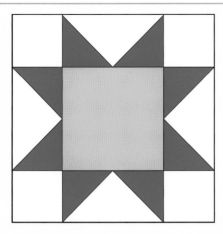

The **sawtooth star** is a quilt block that features four flying geese blocks and four squares surrounding a large central square.

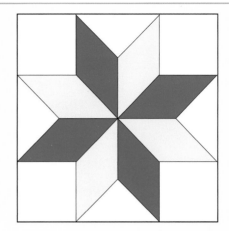

The **Lemoyne star** is one of the classic quilting star blocks. Comprising eight parallelograms set in alternating colors, this star can be used as a single block in a larger quilt or be blown up to make one large star as the entire design of the quilt.

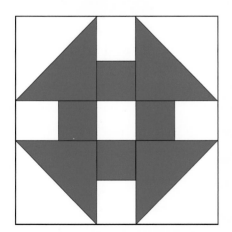

The **monkey wrench** block is another classic example of a simple geometric design that, when set together, can produce beautiful quilts. Consisting of four half-square triangles and four squares, it is an easy block to master.

Anne Sullivan

Initially, I started quilting to express my individuality. I was 8, and I'd learned to sew clothes, but I wanted to do something different than my mom. It turned out that making a quilt took a lot longer than making clothes, and I grew bored. Almost 25 years later, I tried again, and this time I started quilting as a form of creative expression. Instead of getting bored, I got obsessed. Now, after years of quilting, I quilt for many reasons. I quilt for individuality, as a way to differentiate myself from the sameness I still sometimes face in my programming career. I quilt for creative expression, as a way to communicate things that I can't always put into words. And I quilt for community, a group that is important to me and that I am touched to still be part of.

Transcendence, 2015, 36 × 36"

This is Anne's ode to the quilting community. She uses different colors in unexpected ways that work together to create something whole and new. Likewise, Anne says, she is refreshed by the diverse community of modern quilters, with such different backgrounds and interests. Over the years these fellow quilters have pushed her to grow as a designer, a quilter, and a person.

Malka Dubrawsky

I am by nature a maker. I suppose it's a trait inherited from my mother, who never saw a sewn or knitted item she didn't claim she could make herself. That influenced me and, combined with my love of the process of creating, has led to many quilts, garments, home accessories . . . kites. The act of making, though, is only part of the reason I quilt. I love that intangible feeling that comes with using something I've crafted and designed myself. It's an intentionality about what's in my immediate sphere and how I show others love. It's magical.

Clerestory, 2015, 72 × 80"
The sense of a vibrant dappled light in this quilt is much like the light that might come from a clerestory (look it up). Malka's combination of using a single shape and her irregular placement of those rectangles simultaneously conveys a sense of energy and calm, a remarkable feat of design.

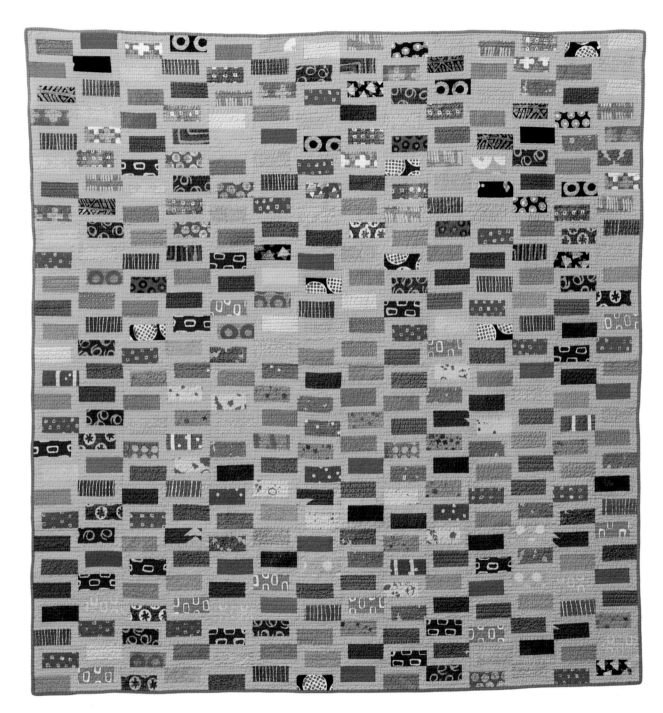

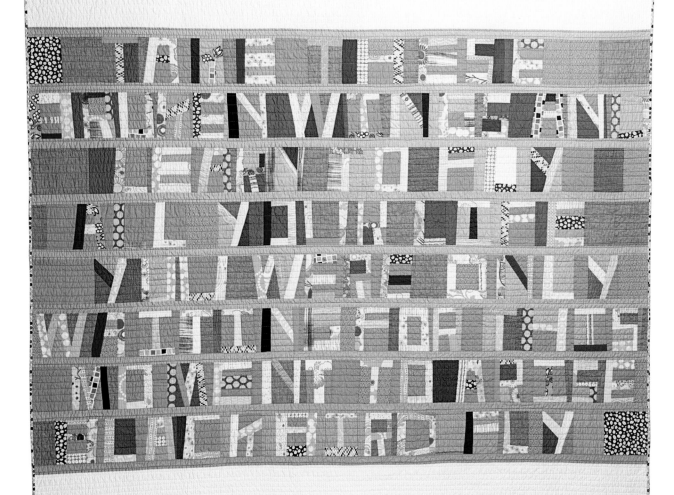

Krista Hennebury

I began quilting 19 years ago as a weekly diversion from the demands of full-time parenting. It immediately became an undeniable passion. In the beginning I quilted to give, but these days I tend to keep more of my work, with the exception of charity or relief quilts. Now I quilt to solve problems, to learn, and to share with others through teaching. I quilt to create beautiful, useful things from fabrics I love. I also quilt to participate in and be part of a creative community. I studied science, not art, so it took me a long time to recognize and accept that quilting is not only my work, it is my place. I love it here.

Blackbird Fly, 2012, 86 × 86"
OPPOSITE: quilt top. ABOVE: quilt back.

MARY FONS

Mary Fons is a wonderful quilter, with one eye looking back and the other looking forward, but what really draws me to Mary is her writing. Since the early 2000s she has been one of the leading writers on quilts and the importance of quilts today. She has the remarkable gift of getting to the core of an issue, the essence of things. Mary is among the handful of quilters that I look to when I am feeling lost.

Memory is an unreliable narrator, but I maintain that my first memory — and not just my first quilt memory but my first memory, full stop — is of sitting on my mother's lap, resting my head on her chest while she hand-quilted on a wooden hoop. We were in a big rocking chair, out on our farm in Iowa. When she spoke, I could feel her voice resonate in her chest. It makes me weep to think of the simplicity and humanity of that scene and knowing how my path and my mother's path went from there is intense for me. That farm scene would disintegrate within a few years with the divorce of my parents, so there's a lot of pain to thinking back to that era. But the rocking chair and the quilt and the mother and the child are completely safe from all that, so it's a sweet memory.

I count as my first real quilt an extremely basic sawtooth star (see page 81) design I made around 2008. For the stars I used a variety of lipstick red fabrics, set on a khaki

Little Black Dress, 2012, 60 × 80"

background. Modern quilting was just starting to be a thing then, so I used all solids. It's the only quilt I have ever made solely using solid fabrics. If I hadn't been so excited to make a quilt, any quilt, I might have abandoned it; it was so flat. I love modern quilts, but I am no modern quilter. I'm a scrap quilter. For me, the more fabrics the better, and I will never again make a quilt without prints. The artistry in printed cloth is my jam.

Given that my mom (Marianne Fons) is a quilt industry superstar, it's ironic that I taught myself to quilt. I grew up in a single-parent household and quilts were what Mom did for work, so quilting did not equal quality time with Mom — though of course my sisters and I grew up with a great love and respect for quilts. But no, the Fons kids didn't learn to quilt as kids, and by the 1990s, almost no one was learning how to sew in school, either.

My experience learning to make quilts is unique: I learned over the years, in real time — on public television and on the Internet. Not by *watching* television and surfing the Internet but *on* those platforms, as host of *Love of Quilting* on PBS and Quilty, online. When, in my late 20s, I expressed an interest in making quilts, the corporation that had recently acquired my mother's quilting company (Fons & Porter) pounced on me. It was good for business to have Fons the Younger put a fresh coat of paint on the brand they had just purchased. No one gave much of a thought to how tough it would be for me to become, hopefully, a "real" quilter in full view of millions of American quilters. But it worked out because I'm strong and smart and — far more importantly — quilts are more powerful than corporations.

Many quilters say, "Quilting keeps me from going crazy," and this is also true for me. Except I don't mean it the way they typically do, which is that the process of making

90

Northbound, 2013, 108 × 126"
This original design relies on one of the earliest traditional quilt block patterns,
flying geese (see page 13).

Quilts cannot be contained. Quilts are tricksters; they shape-shift. Quilts are impossible objects, occupying a space . . . outside a capitalist system of value; . . . outside the ivory tower of Art-with-a-capital-A; and outside of time.

patchwork is relaxing or meditative. For me, it's a little darker than that. I find the world overwhelming, senseless, and absurd. I love it here, but I think about death all the time and about how little time I have left. There are two ways I manage my crushing sorrow and bewilderment: I write and I read about history. These two things, too, can be overwhelming: Write what? And which history? What part? More than anything else, quilts have provided me with an angle, setting me on a path that makes sense. I read about quilt history and thereby learn the history of everything. I write about quilt culture and thereby write about everything. I'm a writer and a historian with a specialty. And this anchors me. From here, I can go anywhere, because quilts are everywhere.

I believe textiles run a *very* close second to food and water when you look at what a human being needs to survive. As long as we have cloth, we will explore and manipulate its properties. We do it for survival until we can do it for art and for love. Not everyone has the money or the time to make quilts. I am fortunate to be able to make them, at least for now, and I will continue to make them as long as I'm able, since as long as I make them, it's proof I'm surviving.

Quilts cannot be contained. Quilts are tricksters; they shape-shift. Quilts are impossible objects, occupying a space outside the patriarchy; outside a capitalist system of value; outside feminism, racism, and class; outside the ivory tower of Art-with-a-capital-A; and outside of time. Quilts are wild animals, and I am proud to be a quilter because I try to be a wild animal, too.

Dashed, 2011, 60 × 80"
In this quilt, Mary mixes subtle color variations with a few boldly colored blocks to give new life to the traditional churn dash block pattern.

VICTORIA FINDLAY WOLFE

Victoria Findlay Wolfe may well be the most prolific quilter on the planet. It seems that every time I blink she has brought us another marvel. I love her densely patterned quilts, constructions that are simultaneously full of energy and history. She seems to draw inspiration from everything, somehow finding beauty everywhere.

I was a child who never ceased to make things.

I was an obsessive coloring-book artist. I picked up twigs and tree branches to make forts and I picked up scraps of wood that I painted pictures on and hung on my walls. If you went back to my childhood bedroom, you'd find watercolors, calligraphy, paper cuts, and screen-printed, homemade posters on my walls for *White Nights*, The Outfield, and Def Leppard. (Don't judge me!) You would find pillows made from leftover bits of fabrics from my father's upholstery business and doll clothes made from scraps from my mother's sewing basket.

When it comes to creating art, I've always been an "overthinker." As a child I had a hard time falling asleep at night because I did not know how to get my brain to stop thinking about all the projects I wanted to make, build, or color. I recall lying in my bed under one of my grandmother Elda Wolfe's scrappy double-knit polyester quilts. With my finger, I would trace the patterns. Like following a magical maze, I would wander from color

The Happy Wanderer, quilted by Shelley Pagliai (designed by Victoria Findlay Wolfe), 2016, 80 × 90"

to color, picking a different favorite each night. This process eventually would calm my brain, and I'd drift off to sleep having colorful dreams, which I swear influence my use of color in my own work to this day.

From watching my grandma stitch, I knew how much work it was to make those beautiful quilts. They were incredibly special and have inspired everything I've done in my own work. My grandma and grandpa lived far enough away that we only got to see them two or three times a year, and I missed them greatly. My love for them is etched into my heart.

ABOVE: Victoria in the studio.
OPPOSITE: *Double Edged Love*, quilted by Lisa Sipes (designed by Victoria Findlay Wolfe), 2013, 66 × 77".
This quilt simultaneously deconstructs the traditional double wedding ring quilt,
yet leaves enough of it intact. It feels to me like a questioning of the simple conventions of love
while remaining an ode to love (and marriage) itself.

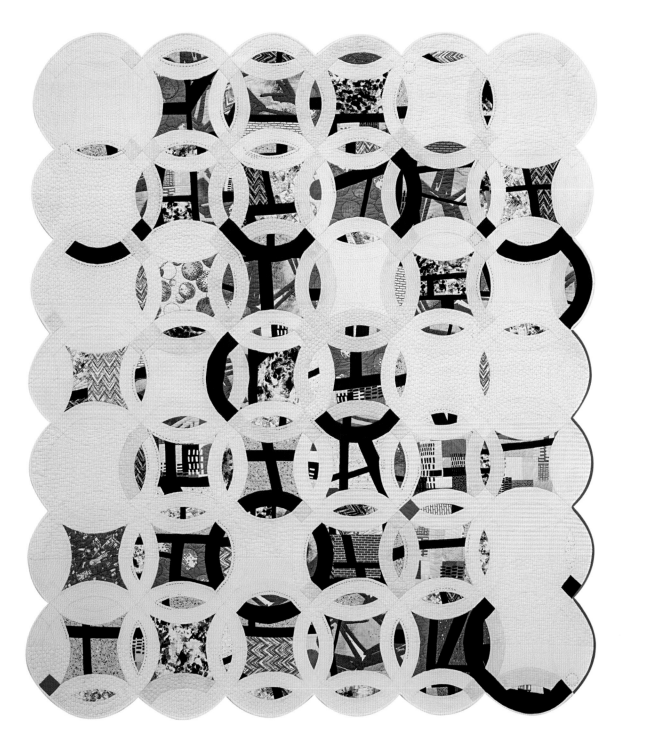

If someone had told me, "Wonky is okay," that might have become a finished quilt.

I learned most of my sewing skills from my mother and father, as they both sewed. I learned hand patchwork in middle school and, with my mother's help, I made Lemoyne stars (see page 81) for my grandmother and aunts one Christmas. Hand patchwork led to appliqué, after which I recall thinking, "I'll never do this again." So I stuck to hand piecing and made a few queen-size quilt tops by hand, and I used them as bedspreads in my first apartments. I never finished them into quilts, as I didn't know how.

One quilt top I recall making, and still have, is an Amish-inspired turquoise and pink bar quilt with monkey wrench blocks (see page 81) in the corners. I got so frustrated with the blocks because I could not make them perfectly, so I abandoned the project. Now I look back at that and laugh. If someone had told me, "Wonky is okay," that might have become a finished quilt. For some that kind of frustration would end a hobby, but I have a hard time passing up a challenge. When I got my own sewing machine in college, I made several more quilt tops.

One of a Kind, quilted by Shelly Pagliai (designed by Victoria Findlay Wolfe), 2018, 90 × 90"
OPPOSITE: quilt top. ABOVE: Victoria designing.

Quilts feel good. They are comfort food for the soul.

I make quilts (and any art, really) out of a challenge to see if I can. I love knowing how things work, how they are built. That discovery process ignites and excites my brain. And that is precisely why I make anything. I get a physical rush from figuring things out. For me, creating is addictive. I make quilts because I need to. I'm still that little kid who can't turn her brain off at night.

For me, quiltmaking is both therapeutic and crazy-making at the same time. I can't not do it (the crazy-making part), and I love the process so much that it's therapeutic. I love making quilts that relate to my happy memories. I can't make a sad quilt. Even if I'm making it for a sad occasion, making it brings me joy and the finished quilt brings comfort to the person who receives it.

Quilts feel good. They are comfort food for the soul. They can be personal, they can be political, they can be a voice, they can be a hug. This has been the case for years before us and will be long after we are gone.

Whether you agree or not:

- Quilts are Art.
- Their makers are Artists.
- The sooner we as quiltmakers embrace that, the sooner the rest of the world will see them that way as well.

- Label your work.
- Be proud of the creative choices you made.
- Someone will love it, even if you don't.

Color Study H1, quilted by Shelly Pagliai (designed by Victoria Findlay Wolfe), 2017, 70 × 65"

CHAPTER 4

WE QUILT TO CREATE A CONNECTION WITH LOVED ONES.

The gift of a quilt is a beautifully selfish gift;
it guarantees that we will remain part of
the recipient's life despite distance and time.

 There are reasons why we give quilts as gifts that go beyond the simple act of sharing our work and the offering of warmth. Each quilt given binds giver and recipient together. No matter where the recipient of a handmade quilt may move, that quilt constitutes an invisible thread leading back to the maker.

In many ways that is the ultimate subtext of all quilts: they represent a desire to be remembered, to remain connected. Every time I use one of the quilts that have been given to me, the maker comes alive to me, entering the room symbolically. Distant friends, even those who have slipped away, remain part of my family through the quilts they have given us. Quilts even have the power to bring back the dead, at least in our imagination. My wife's grandmother is present in our house when we use one of the quilts she passed down to us.

The connections quilts create are enduring things. They are not the fleeting, ephemeral connections of ordinary objects. Because every quilt represents a little bit of the maker's life — including the countless hours given over to making it and the self-expression stitched into the decisions behind every detail — those quilts we give as gifts carry with

> The quilts in our homes all send this same message:
> you are warm; you are safe; you are loved.

them a certain gravity that draws us together. The gift of a quilt is an act of love not because it involves sharing something we have made, but because it is a request, an act of hope that despite distance, giver and recipient will remain connected. That is why I call quilts selfish gifts; they are as much for the maker as they are for those they are given to. They represent our need to be a part of the other's life even if we can't physically be there. Quilts become our surrogates when distance separates us from our loved ones.

Of course, we also make quilts for those nearest to us. For so many, the first quilt they ever make is a baby quilt, reflecting the maker's desire to be the one to keep a newborn warm and safe — and ultimately loved. I think the same impulses apply to the rest of the quilts we make. The quilts in our homes all send this same message: you are warm; you are safe; you are loved.

I suppose this is the central metaphor of the quilt: warmth — once a literal protection against the elements — is also a symbolic means of protection, and our desire to protect is a reflection of the love we feel for another. While quilts given to those remote from us serve as a tether, quilts for our own homes act as insulation against the difficulties and uncertainties of the outside world.

A quilt in progress in Thomas Knauer's studio.

These quilts fulfill our desire to wrap up our loved ones and keep them safe forever. Even though we know we cannot literally do so and that our loved ones must be a part of the great big world, we can at least offer a daily refuge in the form of our quilts, which can provide symbolic shelter against the inevitable trials and tribulations. In the end I

cannot help but see these quilts as something akin to swaddling blankets writ large; they represent that same desire to comfort and protect, to embrace and secure. The quilts that stay in our homes are, ultimately, testaments to our love.

Finally, we make our quilts in anticipation of their being passed down through the generations to come. Of course we make our quilts to be used now, but we cannot help but be aware that quilts have long life spans and that they may well outlive us. And that is part of the beauty of quilts: they have lives of their own and they endure in a world where so much is fleeting.

Just as we use my wife's grandmother's quilts, I can imagine the day when my grandchildren will pass my quilts down to their children, bringing new life to the baby quilts I made for my little ones. As quilts are used they become steeped with memories: slumber parties and picnics, births and marriages. The inevitable spills and stains testify to the life of a quilt and remind us of how intimately our quilts have been a part of our lives. These stories become part of what is shared when we pass down a quilt to the next generation.

As such, quilts can stand as testimony to the quiltmaker's life. They are an autobiography in cloth and thread. Quilts are a legacy we craft for the generations to come; they guarantee a connection across the decades and even across the passage into death. Every quilt evokes its maker, suggests her presence even if she is ultimately absent. In this light it is not just the quilt that endures. The quilter, too, outlasts the constraints of time.

Cinderblocks, Thomas Knauer, 2013, 64 × 82"
In response to log cabin quilts, *Cinderblocks* is based on the ubiquitous building material of my time, transforming that humble object into a joyful quilt that reflects the home.

OTHER VOICES IN AMERICAN QUILTING

While much of this history so far has been about the mainstream of American quilting, some of the most remarkable quilts were made outside of that dominant quilting tradition. These other traditions are no less important to the history of quilting. Indeed, they show just how wide-ranging the practice of quilting has been.

Amish Quilting: Simple but Not Simplistic

The Amish were latecomers to quilting, only really accepting the practice in the closing decades of the nineteenth century. As a deeply conservative religious community, they adopted change carefully, and only if it fit in with the spiritual dictates of the community. So, when Amish communities began quilting, they did so in contrast to the prevailing quilting trends among the "English" (the Amish term for those outside the community). Rather than adopt the complicated

The center square quilt design is one of several iconic Amish quilt designs. With its emphasis on pure simplicity, quilts such as this one reflect the simple life the Amish live. (*Center Square*, maker unknown, circa 1880–1900.)

The bar quilt is another typical Amish quilt from the first half of the twentieth century.
While more complicated than the center square design, quilts like this one nevertheless convey
an essential simplicity. (*Bars*, maker unknown, circa 1900–1920.)

The remarkable quilts of the Old Order Amish communities are publicly sedate, but privately reveal the individual creativity and expression of their makers.

piecing and appliqué of the time, the Amish turned to far simpler designs, most commonly center square patterns, with bar and diamond-in-the-square variations emerging over time (see pages 108, 109, and 130).

Though the designs the Amish produced were consistently simple, they were far from simplistic. Clearly Amish quilters paid attention to proportion. It feels as if those center squares could be of no other size. They also used color in remarkably subtle and sophisticated ways. At times the colors they used in a quilt were so similar that the difference would escape the casual observer. At other times they introduced bright colors, producing extraordinary contrasts.

Finally, though their designs were resolutely simple, the quilting stitches told another story. Amish women had exceptional needle skills and quilted intricate patterns into their minimal quilt tops. Yet their use of dark thread to blend with the rich, deep colors of the fabrics meant that this intricacy all but disappeared, except on close inspection. It is as though their quilts were mimicking their style of dress: Amish women frequently wore brightly colored dresses, but when in public covered these expressions of individuality with black cloaks. Likewise, the remarkable quilts of the Old Order Amish communities are publicly sedate, but privately reveal the individual creativity and expression of their makers.

Though it is tempting to compare Amish quilters with minimalist artists, that comparison can only be of the most superficial nature. While minimalism was the height of modern art during the 1960s and 1970s and pushed the boundaries of art, Amish quilting was fundamentally conservative, a reflection of the spiritual life of the community. These quilts were not simple for the sake of simplicity; they were an embodiment of lives lived simply and dedicated to faith.

African-American Quilting: Beyond Gee's Bend

For far too long African-Americans have been relegated to the margins of the quilting world, regarded as distinctly "other" when noticed at all. Some of this is due to the small number of surviving examples identified as African-American quilts made in the nineteenth century. But it is also important that we recognize that for so many years quilting has been seen as the purview of white women.

In reality, African-American women have been quilting for as long as there has been quilting in America and have made quilts of every style imaginable. Slave seamstresses regularly made technically masterful quilts for the slave owners' use, while at the same time they were making quilts for their own use from whatever was available.

While many of us know of the quilts of Gee's Bend and the Bible quilts of Harriet Powers, it is all too easy to take those well-publicized examples as typical of the whole of African-American quilting. In truth, the quilts made over the centuries by African-Americans run the same gamut as those of white quilters, from *broderie perse*

Much attention has been paid in recent years to the improvisational quilts of Gee's Bend, but to fully understand the scope of African-American quilting we must also recognize that there was a tremendous overlap between mainstream and marginalized quilting communities, at least in the quilts that were being made. (*Alphabet*, maker unknown, circa 1930–1950.)

The quilts made over the centuries by African-Americans run the same gamut as those of white quilters, from *broderie perse* to pure improvisation.

This beautiful example of an axe head (sometimes also known as apple core) quilt rides a line between pattern and improvisation. The quilter strictly adhered to the pattern itself, but improvised the use of color. (*Axe Bit*, Rita Marshbanks, circa 1920.)

to pure improvisation. There are, to be sure, distinctive African-American traditions in quilting — most notably the greater acceptance of improvisation — but the majority of African-American quilts participate in the same trends and practices as those of white quilters.

Though scholarship surrounding African-American quilts is ongoing, popular understanding of African-American quilting too often stops with Gee's Bend. In order to truly see the story of American quilting, we need to incorporate a broader perspective. As long as we continue to assume that the history of American quilting is primarily white, the story of quilting will remain forever segregated.

This improvisational quilt is an excellent example of one current in African-American quilting from the first half of the twentieth century. Quilts such as this reflect a bold approach that ran counter to the rise of quilt patterns. (*Triangles*, maker unknown, circa 1940.)

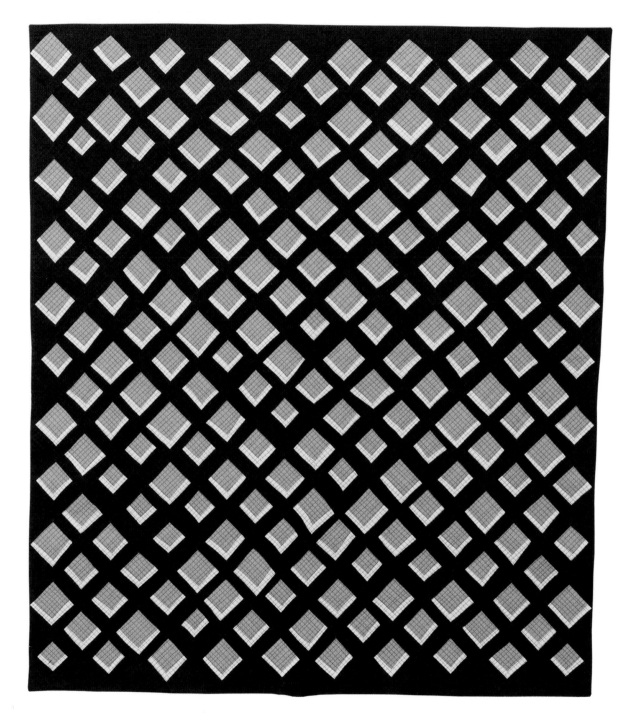

Jill Fisher

I don't think my hobby would have developed into the passion I have today without the grief I experienced at the loss of my little girl Quinn. At a 22-week ultrasound, it was discovered that her heart had stopped beating. With that news, the world lost its sparkle for me and I lost my voice. The one clear memory I have of that time is my labor and delivery nurse holding my hand and apologizing to me that she didn't have a quilt to give me for our baby girl. I surfaced long enough to ask, "Do you need quilts?" "Yes," she replied. "Too many." As soon as I was physically able, I started to work. The repetitive movements of cutting, piecing, and pressing soothed my soul. I found great comfort in participating in the metaphor that quilting is. I could physically put pieces back together into something more beautiful than the sum of the parts. I could share a message of love and an acknowledgment of loss with parents I would never know or have the opportunity to hug. Making those sacred quilts helped me regain and share my voice and see everything a quilt could be.

Rattlesnake, 2017, 39 × 45"

The subtle variations in size of the elements in this quilt transform it into more of a texture than a pattern. Indeed, the dark quilting only serves to heighten that sense of texture as it moves over the lighter colors. Its delicate irregularity produces a wonderful visual effect and circumvents our accustomed ability to slip into an easy pattern.

Casey York

I am a former art history professor and believe that all art can be understood — at least in part — as a means of communication. When I consider why I am motivated to quilt and why the practice gives me joy, I always come back to the same core principle: for me, each quilt is a point of connecting my thoughts and perceptions to the people around me. My quilt and fabric designs are inspired by the things and ideas I encounter in the world, both natural and man-made. And my process of quilting is driven by a desire to share my thoughts and feelings with a larger community. That might comprise a single, beloved gift recipient; a larger group of fellow quilters who share my personal style; or a still-larger audience of viewers who are similarly moved to translate their own ideas into quilted form.

Shards, 2015, 50 × 70"

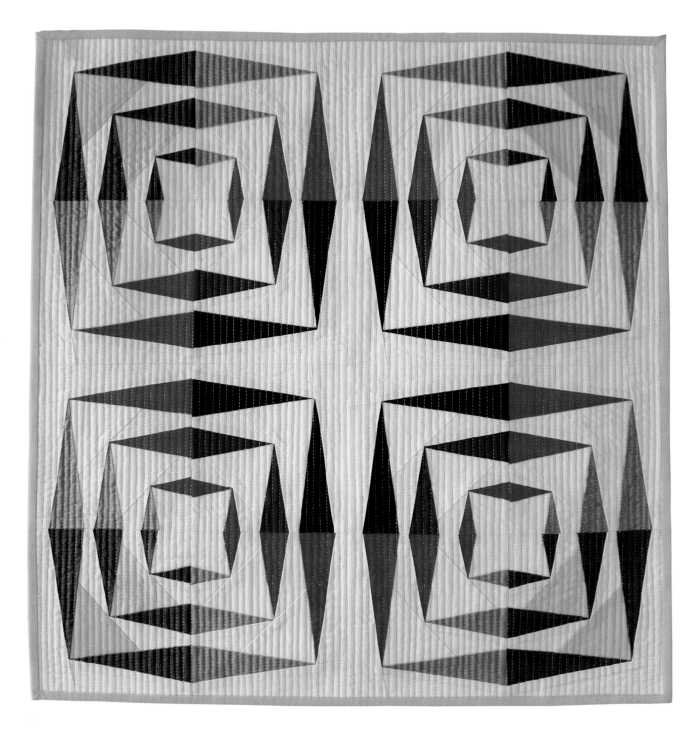

Stacey Lee O'Malley

I started making quilts at a time when I was living far away from family and friends. I think the idea of comfort — through a craft that I could literally wrap around myself — was a large part of why I began. Soon after, I found friends online and in real life through quilting. Participating in the quilt community has driven me to keep making, sharing, and challenging myself.

119

Paper Cut No. 1, 2016, 24 × 24"

Nicole Neblett

I quilt for the satisfaction of creating, of taking my vision for a design and turning it into a product that is both artistic and practical. I quilt to escape the mundane and play with fabric, design, and color, exploring combinations of lines, shapes, and textures. I quilt to leave my daughters a legacy of more quilts than they could ever use and to model for them the pursuit of creative interests with passion and dedication.

Red X, 2015, 31 × 40"

This elegant design firmly differentiates between simple and simplistic. All of the subtle decisions that went into this quilt produce a rich and fully articulated space without overwhelming the eye. It offers both movement and calm, a hallmark of the best minimal designs.

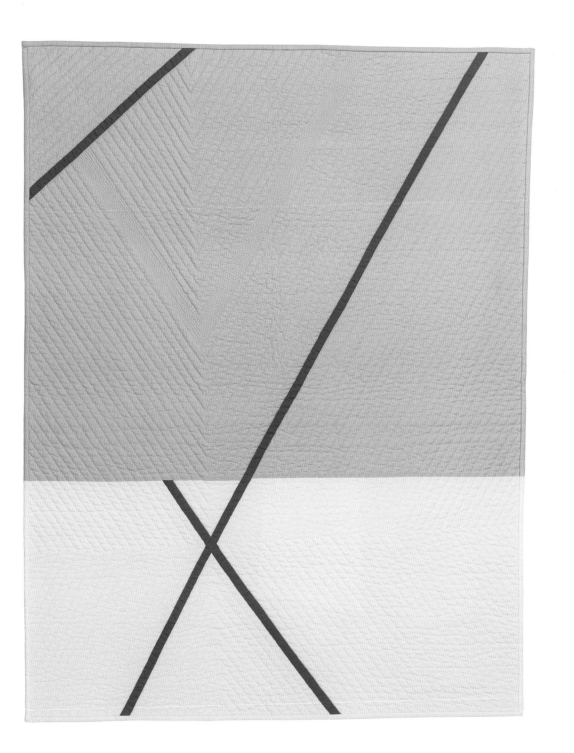

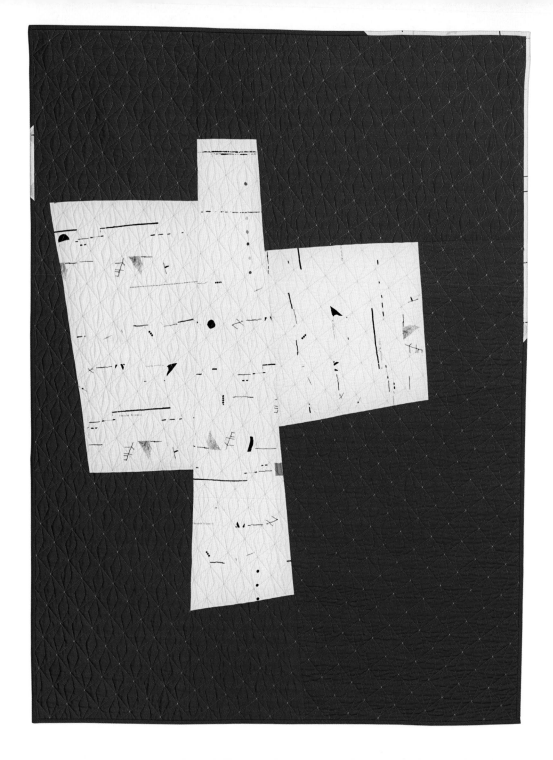

JACQUIE GERING

Jacquie Gering's work beautifully explores the fundamental materials and processes involved in making quilts. I adore the way she sees shapes and spaces, the way she relates her piecing to her quilting, and the remarkable attention to those minute details that make good quilts great. Jacquie is simultaneously humble and confident, intuitive and grounded, and in many ways, I see her quilts as the children of these contrasts. A past president of the Modern Quilt Guild, she is a guiding presence for modern quilting.

123

I see quilts as part of the fabric of the American experience. When I say, "I am a quilter," 99 percent of the time someone tells me their mother, grandmother, aunt, or some distant relative was a quilter or that they own a quilt.

Quilts are familiar and are part of the history of families. Comfort and cuddling don't go out of style. Quilts will always have that role to play, but they also have been and always will be much more than objects of comfort. I don't believe the role of quilts or what quilts mean has changed, but I do think their visibility and accessibility have.

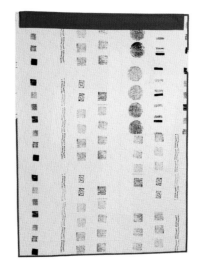

Yoshiko's Cross, 2016, 45 × 60"
OPPOSITE: quilt top. ABOVE: quilt back.

ABOVE: *Geared Up*, 2016, 60 × 60"
OPPOSITE: Jacquie's studio.

My own experience with quilts is a great example. Though I remember quilts from my childhood, I'm not sure I would have known they were quilts if you had asked me then. I wasn't familiar with how they were made or how they may have been different from a typical blanket. For me, they were just blankets.

When I was a young mother in the 1980s, I remember my mom hand-quilting blocks and then putting them together into a quilt for her bed. I thought it was a lot of work for something she could have bought at a department store, though I was in awe of her skill and technique.

Years later, it was my mom who got me started on my first quilt. It was the early 1990s and we were spurred by an article in Martha Stewart's magazine or an episode of her show. My mom loved Martha Stewart and tackled all sorts of projects based on her recommendation. In those years I was a working mom with two active kids and had no time for much else. I don't think I would have attempted the quilting project without encouragement from my mother. It was something we could talk about together, and she was thrilled to see me sewing. I completed the top and then started hand quilting the queen-size quilt. I finished about a third of the quilting, then gave up and let life take over. That quilt sat on the frame for about 20 years.

126

It was 2008 or 2009 before I first finished a quilt. I had quit my job, and after seeing a Gee's Bend exhibit and reading all about those quilters, I stumbled onto Nancy Crow and the budding modern quilt movement. I was intrigued. I decided to make quilts. I took fabric from my mom's cupboard (I didn't own any fabric) and made an around-the-world quilt (see page 130). It had lots of squares, seemed pretty easy, and of course, I hand-quilted it. Didn't everyone hand-quilt? Today I think that quilt is butt-ugly, but I finished it. That was my real entrance into the quilting community and the start of a journey.

This journey has proven to be about far more than making quilts, though. Quilting has allowed me to take risks, grow as a person, and become the artist that maybe I have always been inside. Quilts offer me a medium for artistic expression and an opportunity to find something in myself that I'm not sure I knew was there. I am a teacher by trade

Aftermath, 2013, 40 × 60"
Jacquie Gering tackles issues so concisely without telling the entirety of the story.
With *Aftermath*, we are left to fill in just what this is the aftermath of, and in asking us to do so,
Jacquie forces us to connect some uncomfortable dots.

For me, quilts are personal.
Quilts are life represented.
Quilts are art. Quilts speak.

128

and I'm very good at it. I love my profession but have always felt that I chose it by default. It was what was available, expected, and safe. When I quit my job in 2008, I thought I'd get another job in education. I don't know what sparked in me after my visit to the Gee's Bend exhibit, but that day I told my husband I was going to make quilts.

For more than 10 years now I have worked hard to establish my own voice as a quilter and, at the same time, to learn, grow, and evolve artistically. I love modern art, mid-century modern design, Scandinavian design, minimalism, hard-edge painting, and color-field painting to name a few. When I quilt, I make work that I like personally, so many of my pieces have elements and characteristics of the art and design that I am drawn to. I'm also passionate about several issues, and the quilts I make have given me a way to speak about those issues. For me, quilts are personal. Quilts are life represented. Quilts are art. Quilts speak.

Some quilts are created to have powerful messages: to speak, to provoke, to confuse. But not every quilt has a profound message. Some aren't meant to say anything except it's pretty or it accomplished what I set out to do. I love that I have the opportunity to make all kinds of quilts. Above all, I want my quilts to say "me."

Building Bridges, 2012, 70 × 85"

Variations on the Square

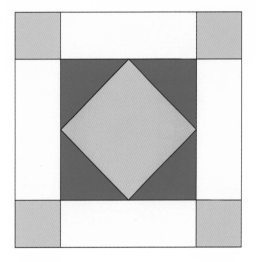

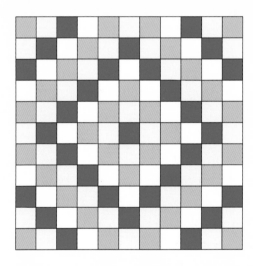

The **diamond in the square** quilt is a traditional Amish design that comes in many variations. The essential element, though, is a single diamond placed within a square in the center of the quilt.

An **around the world** quilt is made up entirely of small squares radiating outward from a center square to produce a diamond within diamond design. These quilts are fairly simple to make but can be quite visually stunning.

HEATHER JONES

Heather Jones is a master of subtlety. Her quilts are powerfully simple, though never simplistic. Space, scale, and proportion are her dominions as she works with an acute eye for color in a space simultaneously reminiscent of the best of Amish quilting and the world of minimalist art. In Heather's quilts there is always a hint of something intangible, something beyond the forms themselves that lends grace to her formal explorations.

131

■

My first memory of a quilt is of the baby quilt that my great-great Aunt Ollie made for me when I was born. It's a nine-patch quilt (see page 42) made out of a pink-and-white novelty fabric, hand-pieced, and tied with yarn, as was Ollie's preferred way of quilting. She was my maternal grandfather's aunt, and she was 84 years old when she made the quilt for me. As a child it was one of my favorite things and continues to be to this day. It has seen lots and lots of use. While I knew Aunt Ollie briefly as a child, I was always struck by the fact that she made me a quilt, by hand, when I wasn't her grandchild or even her great-grandchild. I was just her great-great-niece.

I began collecting vintage and antique quilts as a teenager, but for many years I was quite intimidated by the art of quiltmaking. It looked really complicated and I felt that everything had to line up perfectly. Plus, usable quilts are rather large in size. Other than my great-great Aunt Ollie, no one in my family quilted, so I didn't grow up watching anyone

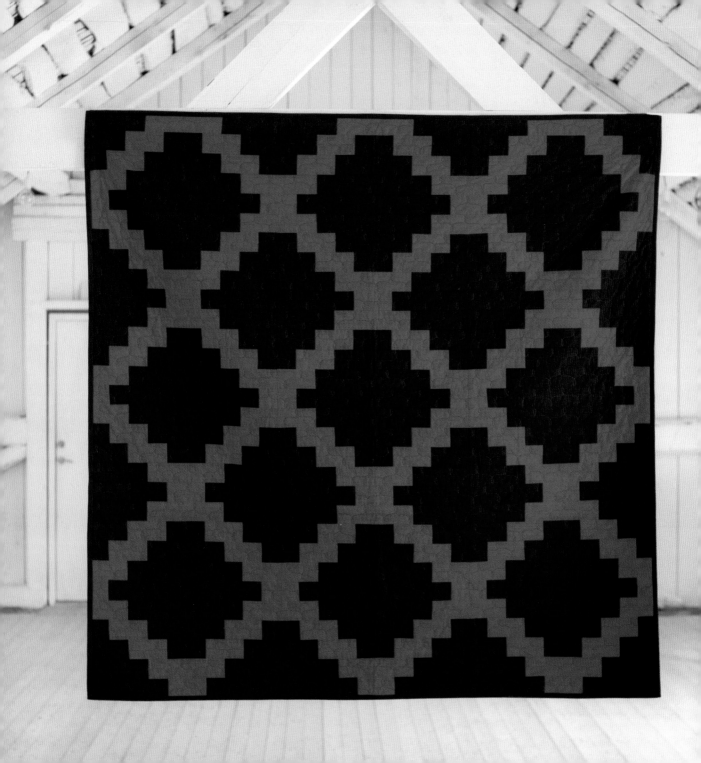

quilt. I finally put my fear aside when I was a junior in college and I made a small lap-size quilt for my mom for her birthday.

Quilts, for me, are primarily an embodiment of love. They are able to provide literal warmth by wrapping a person in cloth and batting. They are also a symbolic token of love, especially when one person gifts a handmade quilt to another.

The main reason I *make* quilts, though, is as a personal creative outlet. Quilts are a means of expressing my designs — those that are planned out and specific as well as those that are more intuitive and improvisational. While I had made a couple of quilts during college, it wasn't until the birth of my first child in 2006 that I began to quilt regularly. Before that I had been a painter, but found myself looking for a cleaner creative outlet. Working primarily with solid colors of fabric felt painterly to me, and I was able to express my creativity with a material that was easy to access, use, and put away when I didn't have much time to devote to an artistic practice.

133

I was always struck by the fact that she made me a quilt, by hand, when I wasn't her grandchild or even her great-grandchild. I was just her great-great-niece.

Central Parkway, 2015, 60 × 60"

ABOVE: *Fly Away*, 2013, 72 × 72". Heather takes simple designs and subtly complicates them. Here, creating a quilt with diagonal symmetry creates a sense of both movement and stability. The solidity of the red square grounds the multitude of half-square triangles (see page 45) that keep the eye moving over the quilt, in effect creating an aesthetic tug-of-war.

OPPOSITE: *Migratory*, 2017, 60 × 80". This original design incorporates elements of the traditional flying geese block (see page 13).

From the beginning, I wasn't interested in copying patterns that I saw; rather, I created my own designs and then figured out how to turn them into quilts. My background in fine art and art history have informed my quiltmaking practice and continue to inspire my designs. Bridging the gap between fine art and craft is important to me. I enjoy gleaning inspiration from works of fine art and translating that into quilt designs. In addition, I find inspiration in the everyday and use that as the starting point for a quilt pattern.

CHAPTER 5

WE QUILT
TO CHANGE
THE
WORLD.

Quilters have long used their quilts
to directly affect the world around them
by raising funds for good works and stitching
deeper meaning into their designs.

I don't think I know a quilter who hasn't donated a quilt to a charity, or a relief effort, or a fund-raiser. It seems to me that this is an essential part of the practice of quilting, to find ways to give back to the world, to allow our quilts to serve a greater purpose. In doing so we fulfill a desire to change some small corner of the world for the better. We use quilting as a barrier against the feeling of helplessness in the face of the injustices we see all around us. We wish we could fix everything but understand that we can't. Instead, we use our skills, our labor, and our time to make quilts that may, in their own small ways, help — whether through raising money or by being given to someone in need.

But in the quilting community, the desire to change the world goes far beyond the model of donated quilts. Indeed, across the wide spectrum of quilting there are quilters making profound statements with their quilts, working through their practice to speak to those who will view their quilts, to advocate for causes and concerns that they hold dear. In many ways this advocacy seems like a natural extension of my belief that every quilt we make is an act of self-expression. Here, however, that expression is more literal, more direct.

By their very nature quilts are filled with meaning —
the meaning of our labor and the unique self-expression
that is stitched into every piece.

It seems so logical that quilters today put their beliefs into their quilts, just as quilters involved in the great social justice movements of the nineteenth century did. When we put so much of our time and labor into our quilts, it seems inevitable that at some point our beliefs and our deeply held convictions will find their way into what we make.

Beneath both of these approaches to affecting the world through quilting lies a more fundamental truth about what we do as quilters. I believe that every single quilt — whether it is given as a gift for a child or as a donation to a favorite charity — changes the world, even in a tiny way. Each quilt we give as a gift strengthens and creates new connections and forms new relationships.

In addition, the quilts we make for ourselves alter how we see the spaces we live in; they fill our households with memory rather than the blank slate of the commercial commodity. By their very nature quilts are filled with meaning — the meaning of our labor and the unique self-expression that is stitched into every piece. In surrounding ourselves with quilts made by our own hands, we mark out a certain type of engagement with the world around us that's based on intimate connections. Ideally that engagement is filled with the joy we feel in making our quilts and the cozy joy that comes from wrapping up in them.

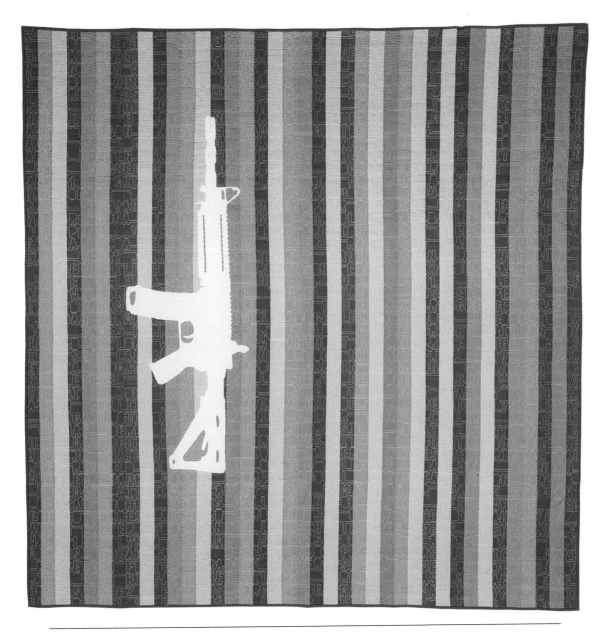

Now I Lay Me down to Sleep, Thomas Knauer, 2016, 76 × 76"
In placing the AR-15 rifle in the place where a partner would lie in a shared bed, this quilt serves as
a critique of the way we seem to prioritize the possession of weapons over human lives. And in
stitching the quilt with names of people killed by guns, in this quilt I draw on traditional quilting's heritage
of shared memories to remind us of the lost futures of all the victims of gun violence.

THE ROLE OF SIGNATURE QUILTS IN REFORM MOVEMENTS

Throughout the nineteenth century, the politics of the day found its way into the quilts women made. Women still could not vote and in many ways were second-class citizens. But they could protest. Women across the continent used quilts, along with other handicrafts, to raise funds for printing pamphlets and sometimes even for bail money. However, to see these signature quilts only as a means of fundraising — in which contributors gave money to include their names (see page 44) — is to miss the radical nature of these quilts.

Signing one's name to a quilt was a public declaration, an act of protest. Considering the resistance many of the reform movements of the nineteenth and twentieth centuries faced from the mainstream, being a public signatory on a quilt was no small act. The quilts themselves were far more than a background for signatures, though; they were enduring statements radically different from a simple petition. Because quilts are large, long-lasting objects, their very material presence lends a certain gravitas to the addition of each signature, transforming the collection of names into an enduring community.

In addition to signature quilts, reform movements — especially the Temperance movement — adopted specific quilt patterns as signals of solidarity. Perhaps the most famous example of this is the Temperance tee pattern (see page 143). Usually executed in blue and white, with T-shaped elements making up the design, this pattern was widely adopted by the Women's Christian Temperance Union.

Though other reform movements did not so readily adopt a particular pattern, individual quilters certainly brought their political causes into the quilts. For example, the antislavery quilt (see opposite) made by a Quaker woman named Deborah Coates includes cloth bearing a common Abolitionist symbol — a praying slave in bondage with the words "Deliver me from the oppression of man" printed below.

Looking at these quilts, it is important to remember that the Temperance and Suffrage movements frequently saw husband and wife divided. Both movements were, at their

Here is a rare example of Abolitionist imagery finding its way directly into a quilt. In the second column from the right, six rows down from the top, the quiltmaker included a small patch printed with an Abolitionist image and logo. See a detail of the patch on the next page. (*Album Quilt*, maker unknown, 1842.)

> Because quilts are large, long-lasting objects,
> their very material presence lends a certain gravitas
> to the addition of each signature, transforming
> the collection of names into an enduring community.

core, protests against male dominance. The Temperance movement was as much about the violent actions of men under the influence of too much drink as it was about alcohol itself. And suffrage was deeply unpopular among many men who wanted to maintain their privileged status. When seen in this context, we can understand that the quilts associated with the various reform movements were not just a means to an end — fund-raising — but were testaments to the resistance, conviction, and fortitude of the women who made them.

This patch of fabric, printed with an Abolitionist image and slogan,
was incorporated directly into the maker's quilt. It is yet another example of how a quilter's politics
worked its way into her quilts. (The full quilt is shown on page 141.)

A Bold Design for a Controversial Cause

143

Temperance tee quilts were often made to be sold or auctioned to raise funds for the Temperance movement. The design itself had many variations, each one involving some arrangement of a T-shaped block.

Hillary Goodwin

As an emergency medicine physician, I feel like I see the best and worst of humanity distilled in my day job. Quilting for me is a meditation of sorts that taps into my artistic brain. It allows me to find peaceful refuge from a tough day. It is an avenue I use to understand and highlight the challenges and tragedies of our human existence.

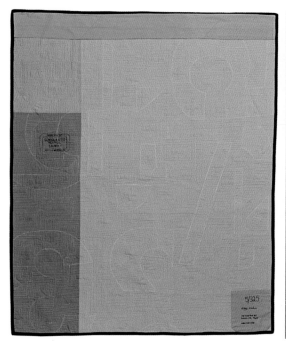

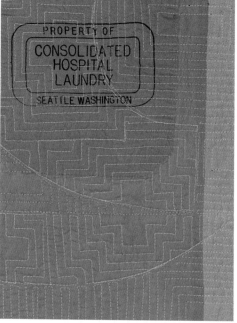

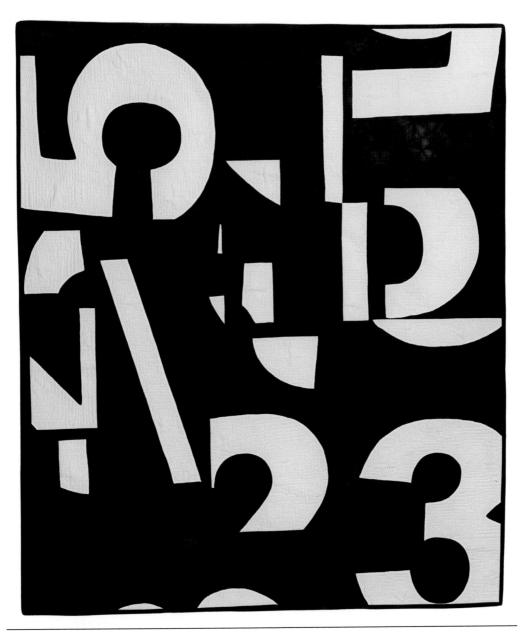

5/325, 2015, 60 × 72"

Kathy York

Quilts help me communicate issues of great importance, in a way that softens the message, hopefully to be heard and thought about and talked about.

My work ranges from women's rights to overdevelopment and protecting the environment — as well as more personal topics like my son's autism. Through my blog and quilt shows and other exhibits, my work has the opportunity to be seen. One piece I made spoke loudly to a woman whose husband had recently died. Just seeing my quilt helped her move forward and do what needed to be done next.

Likewise, quilting is a kind of therapy for me. After my first dog died, I dreamed of him every night for about a year, waking up sad that he was gone. So, I made a photo quilt of him. I made it black and white because dogs see in black and white. I still had his collar and all his rabies vaccination tags and a lock of his hair. I sewed them all on. I cried while I worked on it, but slowly the tears dried up, replaced by happy memories of our fun times together. The process allowed me to move forward.

i Quilt, 2014, 64½ × 62½"

Heather Givans

As an artist, I've witnessed the profound connection that people make with the objects of quilts. They're beautiful. Quilts bring joy. Quilts evoke stories. Quilts are sappy and sentimental. Quilts mark occasions. Quilts express ideas. Quilts are treasures. Quilts express opinions. Quilts give voice. I'm in. I'm all in.

Footnote Quilt, 2016, 62 × 74"
Modulation from bright colors to subtle ones allow this single-block quilt (based on the traditional kaleidoscope pattern) to produce a remarkable amount of movement. While this is in no way a frenetic quilt, I find that it leaves the eye no final resting place, insisting on a perpetual exploration.

CHAWNE KIMBER

Chawne Kimber is one of my quilting heroes. Her deep regard for quilts and the quilting tradition shines through all of her quilts, allowing her to speak with a profoundly authentic voice. Chawne's work is powerful and concise, cutting to the core of whatever issue she is dealing with, whether it's a political statement or a technical challenge.

We grew up with my great-grandmother's quilts on our beds. They were these improvisational utility quilts made from worn-out clothes. Think Gee's Bend. Because the fabrics were already threadbare in places as she pieced the quilts, over decades she repeatedly went back to appliqué patches over the patchwork. Mostly I recall the texture of that sort of make-do preservation. They were also superheavy, likely because she used older quilts for batting, since fresh batting would have been out of financial reach.

I made my first quilt in 2005. I'm a professor, and the sort of hazing process leading to tenure was at a fever pitch for me then. Quilting gave me a refuge where I had control: control of colors, textures, and patterns. That stabilized me. I made 10 quilt tops that academic year just working out the anxiety. Oh, and I earned tenure, too.

I taught myself how to quilt using *Quilting for Dummies*. I'd sewn many body-fitting garments of varying complexity over the years. However, making your work lie flat requires

Bobby Dole's Blue Jeans, 2015, 33 × 33"
This original design is based on the traditional pineapple quilt pattern.

Quilts are also feats of creativity only finished through perseverance and faith — though the slog to finish a quilt is less harrowing than the trek toward equality.

a different set of skills, and I just methodically worked through the projects in the book to learn the basics.

Quilts to me are symbolic of my ancestors' struggles in slavery — involuntarily growing cotton — followed by decades of hardscrabble sharecropping, and then the ongoing grappling for civil rights and human dignity in the United States. That is, quilts are still an organic product of field labor — though many people still turn a blind eye to that labor stream. Quilts are also feats of creativity only finished through perseverance and faith — though the slog to finish a quilt is less harrowing than the trek toward equality.

I make quilts in at least two different genres: abstract geometric studies and meditations on social justice issues. The geometric quilts keep me grounded in the tradition of quilting and help hone my technical skills, while I apply those skills to ensure the structural integrity of all that I make. The works in which I address social issues are motivated by a need for a

ABOVE: in the studio. OPPOSITE: *Cotton Sophisticate*, 2015, 72 × 72"

ABOVE: *The One for Trayvon*, 2013, 38 × 57"
OPPOSITE: *The One for Eric G*, 2015, 79 × 77". Chawne's quilts are extraordinarily direct; she says exactly what she means and minces no words. At the same time, she is incredibly subtle with her designs; in this case, the last repetition of "I can't breathe" staggering downward produces the awful effect of a final breath.

different sort of meaning in the hours that I spend on quilting. Intended to educate, these quilts, when exhibited, expose audiences to perspectives often new to them. As a result, these quilts often start conversations that are fundamental to processing who we are and who we want to be as a nation.

It's important to mention, though, that not every quilt needs to "say" something. There is still a need for quilting just for the sake of it. It's a valid choice that most quilters make — even most art quilters, in fact. However, I do choose to have some of my quilts speak for me. Whether it's a ham-fisted challenge of censorship through expletives splashed on a quilt top or through a two-tone appliquéd memorial for Trayvon Martin, my quilts are simple entry points into issues we face in our culture.

In the end quilting is about the comfort, glory, and honor of craftsmanship to me. And when this becomes irrelevant in our society, we have much bigger problems to address.

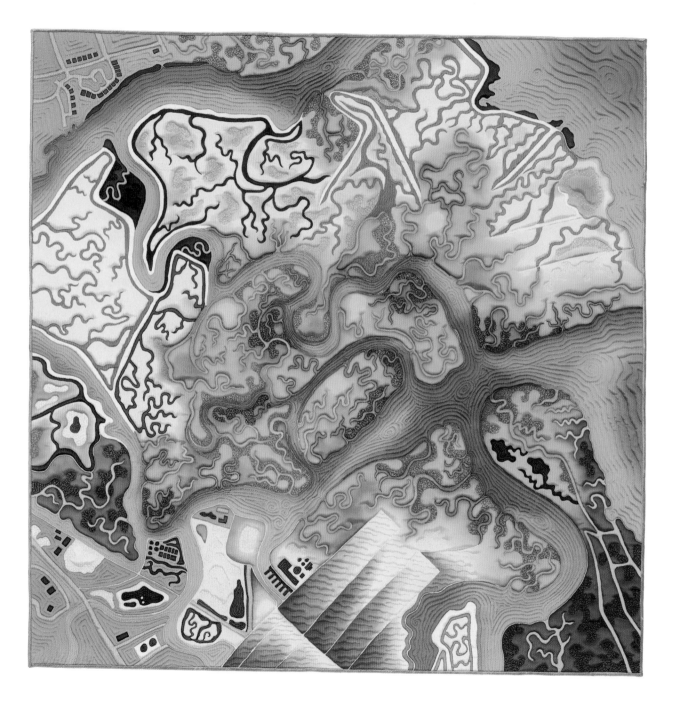

LINDA GASS

There is a beautiful logic in the quilts of Linda Gass, and they simply make sense to me. By using quilting to emulate topographic maps, she is able to make quilts that address the environmental issues with which she is so deeply concerned. For her, quilts are statements that speak in ways other media never could. Linda relates uncomfortable truths through a medium we generally equate with comfort. In her contrast of medium and message, she has found a clarity of voice that is rare.

I make my stitched painting quilts because I want to raise awareness about water- and land-use issues in California and the American West. I want my work to be widely accessible, and the textile medium is something everyone is familiar with. From the moment we are born, we are wrapped in textiles. We wear them and live with them in our homes. Everyone has experienced them. As such, it's an unintimidating art medium different from oil painting or bronze sculpture.

In particular, the quilt medium has several qualities that emphasize and help to convey the landscape aspect of my work. I use a high-loft batting in my quilts so that when I stitch them, I'm effectively sculpting a topographic relief. The luminosity of the silk fabric and the vibrancy of the silk dyes I use allow me to make work that is beautiful. I

Wetlands Take Over, 2013, 30 × 30"

I . . . use the lure of beauty to encourage people
to look at the difficult environmental issues we face.

then use the lure of beauty to encourage people to look at the difficult environmental issues we face.

Growing up in Los Angeles during drought years made me aware of the preciousness of water. That realization has turned into a passion for incorporating water-related concerns into my art. I am inspired by the connections between humans and the water and land that sustain us. In my work, I visually juxtapose environmental vulnerability and resilience, past human memory and future possibilities. I hope to inspire people to care for their water resources and take action.

Quilts were not something I grew up with. My maternal grandmother liked to embroider and sew, and my paternal great-grandmother was a master seamstress. We had no family traditions of quilting, though, and we did not own any quilts. It wasn't until I was in my early 30s that quilts caught my attention. I started seeing modern quilts hanging on the walls of fabric stores, and I was fascinated by them. I found the combination of design, composition, color, and texture very inspiring, but it never occurred to me to make one myself until I started silk painting in my late 30s.

I made my first quilt in 1998. It was part of my progression of finding a satisfying medium to work in as an artist. I had been painting watercolor landscapes and still lifes when I went to a hands-on silk painting demonstration at an art store. I picked up the brush loaded with translucent silk dye and touched it to the silk and was mesmerized watching the dye flow into the silk. I was hooked!

Owens River Diversion, 2012, 45 × 30"

Linda's work is remarkably evocative, never giving away the story but guiding us toward a sense of loss.

In this quilt we are presumably presented with the flora affected by one of many water diversion projects. Linda asks us to see the small in the large, and simultaneously the largeness of this small thing.

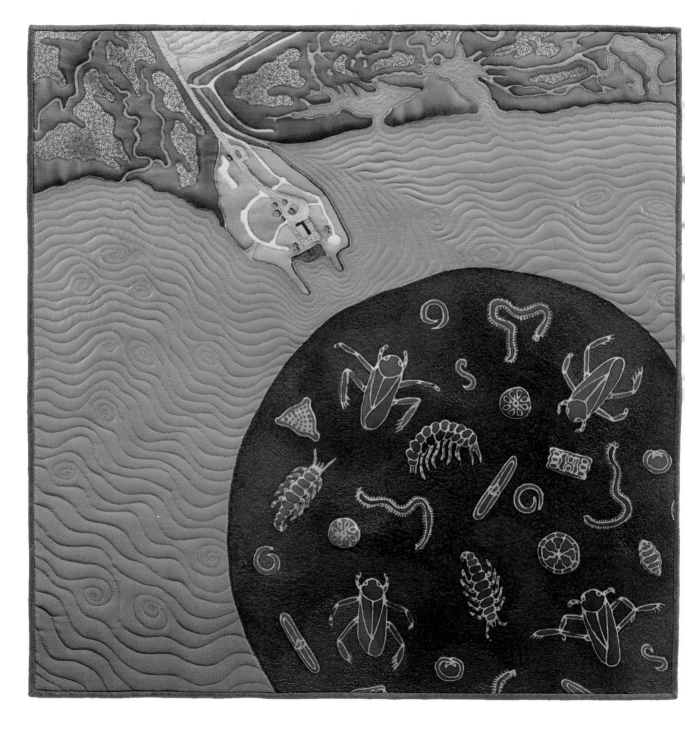

I realized that it was like painting watercolors on fabric, and that opened up a whole new set of possibilities for me: since I enjoyed sewing my own clothes, I decided I could also create my own fabrics! Eventually I turned my focus to making wall art from the silk paintings, and there was something about the linear nature of silk painting that begged to be quilted. That was the inspiration I needed to finally learn to quilt.

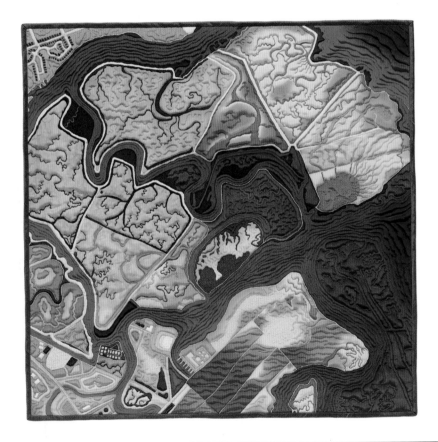

OPPOSITE: *Cooley Landing: Life in Water*, 2015, 18½ × 18½"
ABOVE: *Puzzle of Salt*, 2005, 29½ × 28½"

I started by taking a hand-quilting class at a local quilting store. Although I love the look of hand quilting, I was frustrated by how large and uneven my stitches were, and by the amount of time it would take me to master this skill. I also realized that my life was not long enough to be able to hand-quilt all the ideas I had.

Next I tried a machine-quilting class, where I learned to piece fabric and do straight stitch and free-motion quilting. That class taught me the basic skills I needed to start machine quilting my silk paintings, and the rest of my skills are self-taught, learned through trial and error. For example, I learned early on that machine quilting silk requires planning ahead and focused concentration to stitch the silk only once. Because the sewing machine needle makes an irreparable hole in the fabric that will always be visible, you want to avoid having to rip out unwanted stitches. Once I mastered the basic skills, I created my first machine-quilted silk painting.

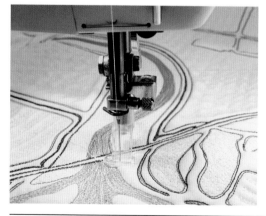 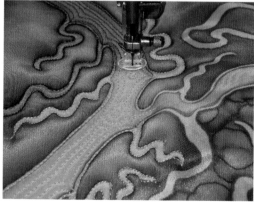

ABOVE: in the studio, stitching through silk and high-loft batting.
OPPOSITE: *San Joaquin Merced Revival*, 2012, 45 × 30"

For me, the process of quilting is meditative, immersive, and creative. The final result embodies care and mastered craft, and it's the physical manifestation of my desire to care for, restore, and repair our damaged environment.

I'm happy to see that quilting is one of the methods enjoying a renaissance in today's "maker" movement. Making quilts satisfies that basic human impulse to create. And today's modern quilts don't even need to be made from fabric or stitched together with thread: makers have the freedom to use the concept of a quilt to create objects from a variety of materials. These exciting possibilities will keep quilts relevant in our ever-changing world.

CHAPTER 6

WE QUILT BECAUSE WE CAN — AND BECAUSE WE CANNOT HELP BUT DO SO.

One of the beautiful things about quilts
is that there need be no other reason to make one
than that we find pleasure in the process.

While there are so many reasons why we quilt that relate quilting to the world around us, I'm not sure there always needs to be a reason to quilt. Regardless of the pressures we may put on ourselves in our individual practices, quilting is a luxury, an indulgence of time that we may not really have to spare.

That is one of the beautiful truths of quilting: it forces us to slow down for a time, to engage in something other than the mundane routines of daily life. The vast majority of us make quilts not because we have to, but because we want to. Each of us has the skills, so we put them to use. I have yet to meet a quilter who doesn't have a Why Not quilt, one made purely because it could be made.

I believe there is something profound in this, something remarkable about the fact that hundreds of thousands of people take time out of their lives to make quilts, whatever their motivation may be. At times the reasons why we quilt may be complex, but beneath it all is the simple truth that we make quilts because that is what we do. There is something liberating about this relationship between person and practice. It is not so much an escape from the world as a settling into a corner of it that we know so well, and that seems to know us.

While some of us enjoy relaxing into the pleasure of quilting, for some of us, quilting feels almost like a calling, even a compulsion.

While some of us enjoy relaxing into the pleasure of quilting, for some of us, quilting feels almost like a calling, even a compulsion. There is something deeply compelling about working with one's hands to make something that will last generations, that will be used and loved. While quilting can be endlessly frustrating, it still speaks to us as something that matters, that somehow makes a difference.

Perhaps we quilt because it gives us structure for accessing our creative sides, but I think there is something more to the call of quilting. Quilts hold an almost mythological place in the American psyche; they stand as a constant in an ever-changing world. Quilts themselves haven't changed much over the centuries, even as technological innovations have altered our methods. We still see quilts as metaphors for security and stability, offering both literal and figurative warmth; this symbolism continues to call us to the tradition and keep us involved in the practice of quilting.

Vows, Thomas Knauer, 2014, 80 × 80"
The piecing of this quilt spells out the final line of the traditional English wedding vows, "And thereto I plight thee my troth," in Morse code, while the quilting writes the complete vows, again in Morse code.

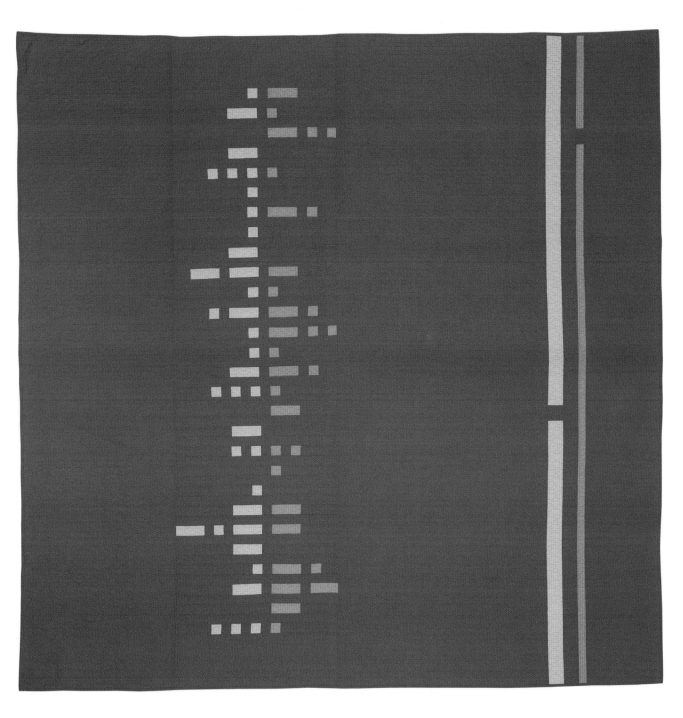

A PIECE OF HISTORY
THE AMERICAN BICENTENNIAL AND QUILTING'S GREAT REVIVAL

In the years surrounding the American Bicentennial in 1976, major exhibits at the Whitney Museum of Art and the Smithsonian, a renewed appreciation of American history, and, to no small degree, Bonnie Lehman's *Quilter's Newsletter* ushered in a genuine quilting revival. Quilting shed its associations with Depression-era poverty and was recast as an essential component of the American experience.

But this revival was different from the ebbs and flows of interest in quilting in the past. Now new quilters were explicitly looking backward through the history of quilting for inspiration and taking inspiration wherever they found it. It was an essentially modern practice of looking backward from the present. This new wave of quilters could jump from period to period, style to style, as they reconnected with the tradition.

Just as Depression-era quilting set the stage for the postwar decline, quilting's relative absence from mainstream culture in

This first issue of *Quilter's Newsletter* from 1969 was the beginning of a new era in quilting, which saw the rise of a mass media surrounding quilting and ultimately the formation of today's modern quilting industry.

These examples of Bicentennial quilts show a range of styles and techniques. CLOCKWISE FROM TOP LEFT: The machine-pieced map is hand- and machine-appliquéd with cottons, velvets, and felted wools (Barbara McKie, 1976). The original star design is made with polyester fabrics (maker unknown, circa 1976). Each square is hand-painted and hand-quilted (Rebecca Thompson, quilt top finished in 1976; quilting finished 2016).

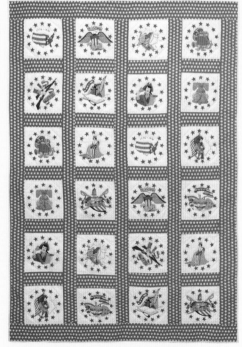

the 1950s and 1960s provided distance that facilitated an explosion of quilting. Countless strains of quilting grew out of this widespread revival. Modern quilting included everything from reproduction quilters intent on restoring the traditional practices to art quilters who stretched the boundaries of what a quilt could be. While the revival may have begun as a fad, it ultimately took root and laid the groundwork for decades of growth as well as the global quilting community of today.

Amy Garro

As someone who started sewing at a young age, I could write that I quilt because the women in my family quilt, because it's a family tradition, or because I love sewing useful objects for others. But while those things may all be true, they are the reason I *started* to quilt; not the reason why I *continue* to quilt. I return to my sewing machine tirelessly, even throughout creative droughts and busy seasons of life, because I find a cathartic release in quilting. The methodic — and sometimes monotonous — process provides a rhythmic, almost ritualistic, backdrop to my life. In contrast, the design aspect of quilting allows for mental freedom and exploration in a purely visual element. I can leave behind the cares and worries of day-to-day life and immerse myself in this place of freedom.

170

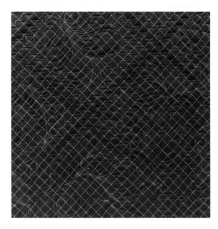

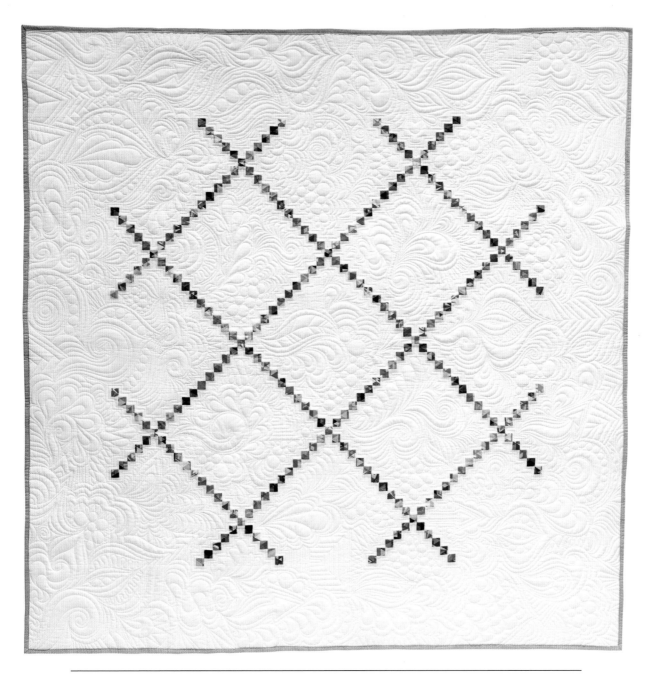

Tamed Geometry, 2017

OPPOSITE: details of back. ABOVE: quilt top.

Latifah Saafir

I quilt
because
I have to.

Convergence, 2013, 60 × 72"

Jolene Klassen

In the beginning, I did not choose quilting; it chose me.

My first job was at the local quilt shop, and in fact I did not even apply for the job. They reached out to me, asking if I would be interested in working part-time. I was 17. I worked there for five years and, in the process, learned all the basics of quiltmaking. I feel that quilting is the best meeting of the practical and artistic worlds. To see the colors and textures of fabric, to join them into pleasing patterns, to mold them into a big, soft, three-dimensional object that can be used for warmth and comfort is the ultimate satisfaction.

Abstract Sister of Modern Prisms, 2015, 47 × 55"
The simultaneous structure and freedom that makes up this quilt is remarkable.
While the individual parts are very simple and do follow a basic geometry, the plays of improvisation
that pop up here and there lend a vibrancy to the quilt that belies its orderly nature.

Brigitte Heitland

Quilting is a world made for me. For years I was on a journey trying this craft or that and getting bored after exploring all the possibilities the craft seemed to offer. With quilting I finally found my true passion. It is as if I open a door only to find that there are 10 more doors behind that I can open and explore. I could go into the world of art quilts or play around with improvisational quilts. I could train my piecing skills with challenging traditional blocks or get out of my color comfort zone and try on new schemes and combinations. I feel that my lifetime will not be enough to go every possible way this textile art leads me. I don't get tired of playing around with new fabric collections and quilt layouts and projects. Can you sense my enthusiasm?

Grey Labyrinth, 2015, 60 × 60"

Jennifer Sampou

I've been designing quilting cottons since 1989 and have thousands of prints in my portfolio. I've been surrounded by quilters for 30 years but really didn't start calling myself a quilter until more recently, when I began to use my own prints in earnest. Although I have loved sewing my entire life — clothes, home decor, baby quilts, and a few large quilts — I had never impressed my inner artist with any of my quilts. Until *Octagon Shimmer*. *Octagon Shimmer* was a breakthrough for me: I had finally put the time and creative energy into making something I was completely proud of. In addition, my three boys are all older now and I actually have more time to create! So, part of the reason I quilt is just a matter-of-fact thing: the gift of time.

179

Octagon Shimmer, 2016, 70 × 86"
Jennifer incorporates a subtle variation on the traditional flying geese quilt block (see page 13) along the top and bottom horizontal strips of this quilt.

Jen Carlton Bailly

180

I started quilting after my daughter was born five weeks premature. While in the neo-natal intensive care unit, she received a beautiful quilt that inspired me to teach myself to quilt. Thank goodness for Google and all those bloggers who turned up in my search of "How to make a modern-day quilt." I had no idea of the rabbit hole I was about to go down. Quilting has become everything for me. It is my time alone with myself. It's a way to express my artistic side. It's my philanthropy. It's how I show my love. It's the best and most loved job I've ever had. It's given me some amazing friends. Really, quilting is who I am now.

Oregon Coast, 2016
This quilt is a beautiful example of how color and shape can speak to something much larger.
Here the merging and enfolding of colors give us the sky and the sea, the vibrancy of a place at
a particular time, the sharing of a memory through fabric and form.

No Value Does Not Equal Free, 2014, 72 × 72"
ABOVE: quilt top. OPPOSITE: detail.

Molli Sparkles

The first quilt I made was about honoring my grandmother. However, like most other quilters, I had plans for my next five creations before the first was even completed. The driving force for me is the tactile experience of working with my hands that culminates in a usable creation. I'm naturally a goal-oriented person, so participating in the many stages of creating a quilt feeds this desire for accomplishment.

So why do I quilt? It taps into my familial history, complements my persona, and continues to challenge and inspire my creativity. Quilting acts as a personification of everything that is important to me. The real question is, how could I not?

183

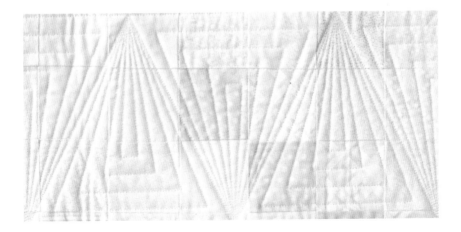

MARIANNE FONS

What can be said about Marianne Fons that hasn't already been said? She is one of the true pioneers of the quilting industry, an absolute giant in the field: half of my sewing studio is stocked with Fons & Porter tools. She is an exceptional quilter who has taught a generation and more how to quilt — while also reminding us why the quilts we make matter.

The quilt that got me interested in making quilts was on the cover of a magazine in a doctor's office waiting room in 1976. It was a pictorial quilt made to commemorate the American Bicentennial. I was a young mother and had been doing embroidery as a pastime, but the bold brush of quilt design appealed to me more than the tiny lines of embroidery thread. I liked the idea of coming out with something larger for the amount of time spent. So when I made my first quilts in my mid-20s, it was to explore and expand the joy of making that I had discovered in constructing my first few blocks.

Once I became aware of quilts as something a person could make, I visited the Iowa State University Extension office on the town square in Winterset, Iowa, and asked for a class. The Extension home economist found a teacher in a nearby town, a notice went in the local paper, and the four-session class filled up. We learned to make templates from cardboard. My cardboard came from diaper boxes.

American Pie, 2017, 84 × 84"

The Fons & Porter mission was to make quilting as enjoyable to our customers as it was to us.

In that class I met my future business partner, Liz Porter; we were younger than everyone else by 5 to 10 years. Liz and I began teaching locally as a team and coauthored our first book, *Classic Quilted Vests*, in 1982. Eleven years later we published *Quilter's Complete Guide*, which became one of the best-selling quilting books of all time and has often been called the "bible of quiltmaking." We both taught quilting classes all over the United States for more than 20 years and eventually were on public television nationwide. We also owned the most popular quilting magazine in America — and all from little Winterset, Iowa.

As half of what became the Fons & Porter brand, my goal was to design mainstream projects that other quilters would want to make so they'd buy our books, patterns, and magazine. As a mainstream quilter myself, I knew that what looked good to me on my design wall would also appeal to other quilters. The Fons & Porter mission was to make quilting as enjoyable to our customers as it was to us.

In my commercial years, I gave few quilts away because they were the tools of my trade, but since the sale of our business in 2006, I have experienced the joy of giving more and more quilts away. I have become closely involved in the Quilts of Valor Foundation,

Checkboxes, 2012, 58 × 69"
This quilt incorporates the album block pattern, which was popular throughout much of the nineteenth century in the United States.

188

serving on its board of directors for seven years and writing for its newsletter. Quilts of Valor are awarded to military service members as a way of saying "Thank you for your service."

Ultimately, I believe, the joy of making is a basic human joy, as is the joy of giving. Nothing says "I love you" like a quilt. Just as loving arms can be wrapped around a baby, a child, an adult, a veteran, so can a quilt.

ABOVE: Marianne designing.
OPPOSITE: *New Hampshire Nights*, 2016, 66 × 94". Marianne makes quilts that feel traditional and evoke the history of quilting, yet at the same time feel timeless. What I love most about her quilts is the way I am rewarded for spending a little more time with them by finding a design detail that originally eluded me. Whereas some quilters might just have lines intersect, for Marianne those spaces are places for new elements to emerge, new details to play.

SHERRI LYNN W

Sherri Lynn Wood's quilts are truly a marriage of process and material, with the des[...] often than not emerging as a by-product of the way she works. It takes a certain leap of faith[...] follow through on the ideas behind Sherri's quilts, to trust that the quilt will work out because the concept, the process, and the material choices are all firmly grounded. I love that as a viewer I can see everything that went on behind the scenes, right there on the surface of the quilt. Here, she adds her unique voice, giving us a behind-the-scenes view of why she quilts.

For me quilts are about relationships, community, home, intimacy, caring, love, expression, collaboration. Quilting is a relational activity that can serve as a model or practice for living. Let me explain what I mean.

In my own quilts I focus on improvisational processes and flexible patterns because I find doing so satisfying and revelatory. The act of creating improvisational patchwork reveals my limits, habits, patterns, and the ways that I make relationships in my life. Behind any improvised quilt is a metastory about the maker's rhythm of attention and the way the quilter makes choices.

My first memories of quilts involve a much more traditional process. When I was 10, I stayed at the family farm in South Hill, Virginia, of a friend and coworker of my dad's.

Linda Susan Wood (1943–2003), 2006, 68 × 62"

The women of the family took me to a quilting bee at the neighbor's farm. I was amazed to see the quilting frame lowered from the ceiling. I wasn't allowed to actually do any quilting, but they did let me wax the threads and thread the needles. Back at the house where I was staying, in the dining room, there was an old Singer Featherweight set up, with stacks of calico triangles or squares, where I could chain-piece patches for future quilts whenever I felt like it.

I really began sewing when I was 12 and was mostly self-taught. I made my first quilt, which was a tied checkerboard quilt (see page 196), for a friend's wedding when I was 24. When I started quilting, I joined a traditional guild in Chapel Hill, North Carolina. I learned a lot of quilting basics and history from the ladies in the guild.

Behind any improvised quilt is a
metastory about the maker's rhythm of attention and
the way the quilter makes choices.

Sol Lewitt/Score for Floating Squares, 2016
As part of an installation piece, Sherri invited participants to interpret and execute a patchwork score for
floating squares based on a mathematical algorithm inspired by the art of Sol Lewitt.

Personally, I see my improvisational work in the quilting community as embedded social practice. It's politically subversive to give people the tools to access their own authority and preferences, particularly within a community that is mostly inclined toward aesthetic perfection and harmony, of implementing well-designed fixed patterns, often mapped out by other people.

Improvisational patchwork, on the other hand, teaches us about systems and how the limits of systems can support or thwart change, variation, diversity, growth, and transformation of ourselves and society. I'm glad to be a part of the broad spectrum of people who are mining the richness and meaning of this medium and art form.

OPPOSITE: *Make Do Improv Round Robin*, 2017

ABOVE: *6 × 4, or Six Pairs of Pants*, 2016, 115 × 98". In her quilts Sherri often leaves hints as to the original purpose of her repurposed fabrics. Here we find pant legs making themselves visible amid an abstract, improvisational design. It is that tension of past use and current incarnation that makes us think about the nature of quilting and the odd insistence on perfectibility in the quilting community.

Alternating Colors, Single Shape

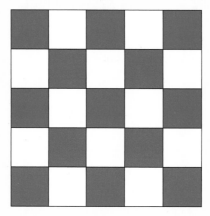

Checkerboard quilts look pretty much like you would expect them to: a field of squares set in alternating colors, or a range of colors alternating with a neutral. While checkerboard quilts may be simple designs, they can produce wonderful effects in the right hands.

ALISSA HAIGHT CARLTON

I love Alissa Haight Carlton's use of color. At times subtle and at other times striking, the way she deploys color across her quilts is, always, spot on. Her quilts often take on a minimal structure, leaving all the more room for her wonderful color studies. And as one of the founders of the Modern Quilt Guild, Alissa brings to her quilting a unique perspective on the way quilts have been seen and transformed over the past decade.

As a kid growing up in rural New Hampshire, I'd been incredibly crafty. I'd participated in 4-H, and there were amazing artisans around to teach me. But I'd stepped away from making throughout high school and my 20s.

In 2007, I was living in Los Angeles, working in television, and was recently married. I had a conscious sense that my work and social life were full and rich, but something was lacking. I was actively looking for something new and more to add to my life. A lot of people were starting to knit then, and I did the same. I turned to the Internet for inspiration and found Flickr. There I saw my first modern quilts. It was the first time it even occurred to me that I might be interested in getting a sewing machine. But I got one, joined in on some block sewing that was being blogged about online, and then dove into my very first (horrible) quilt. It's out there somewhere in all its brown and pink glory.

My skills and craftsmanship have grown stronger by doing things over and over and over again.

There were multiple quilts in my childhood home that were made by people in my father's family. A red-and-white one hung in the kitchen, and I remember a big white-and-pink appliqué quilt on my parents' bed. My mother made a series of quilts when I was in high school, but my quilting skills are mostly self-taught. I used online tutorials and books. I can still very clearly picture all of the photographs on binding in *Denyse Schmidt Quilts*. It was the way I learned how to bind.

From there, my skills and craftsmanship have grown stronger by doing things over and over and over again. Making a lot of quilts is the single biggest thing that has taught me to be a better quilter. Now I continue to learn all the time, and with many quilters among my closest friends, we are always learning from one another.

I have never had a practice like I have had with quilting. I've spent more time making quilts than I've spent on any other craft, hobby, passion, or whatever you're going to call the love of doing something. Quilts have become incredibly important to me personally. And, at my job running the Modern Quilt Guild, I am always immersed in quilts.

My own quilts reflect my personal design tastes. I love simple, graphic design that is then softened (and, I think, made more appealing) by fabric. That balance of hard, stark

Bias 4, 2015, 60 × 75"

design mixed with soft, natural textile really appeals to me and fuels my work. I feel a connection to all other quilters, past and present, through our love of this craft, but I don't try to say anything bigger than that with my work. That might change for me in the future, but for now I'm simply trying to creatively express myself through the design and making of my quilts.

I believe quilts are still relevant because they, like all art forms, allow people to express what they like or feel. Quilters have expressed 2018 in ways as surface as color trends and as profound as the feelings raised by the current political climate. I'd argue that all of these expressions are connected: all art being made today in some way reflects, expresses, and is relevant today because it's made in the hands of today's quilters.

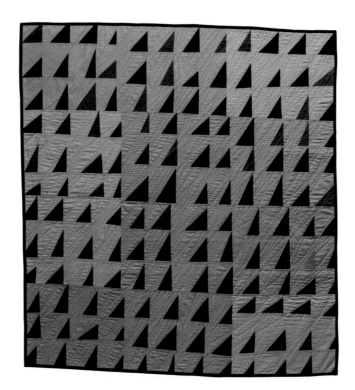

ABOVE: *Intersections*, 2012, 60 × 75"
OPPOSITE: *Didn't Get the Memo*, 2013, 45 × 49". Alissa's deviations are both subtle and
not-so-subtle: her quilts seemingly set up a pattern or a rule, and then systematically deconstruct
that rule. Here a set of triangles becomes a rich vocabulary of form, but one that is made to
feel self-consistent by the single outlying red triangle. For Alissa, difference comes in
degrees, which is what allows for such depth in her designs.

WE QUILT FOR ALL THESE REASONS AND MORE.

Whatever the reason we are initially
drawn to the practice, quilting seems to satisfy
something deep inside, to touch us,
and to allow us, through our quilts, to share
with the people in our lives.

 Now that I have begun quilting, I cannot imagine not quilting. This sentiment is not only true for me; it's one that I have heard countless times as I've traveled within the quilting world.

We quilt because there are quilts yet to be made, gifts still to be given, messages that remain unspoken. We quilt because there are always new babies and more weddings. We quilt because we need to do something with our hands and our minds. We quilt because we need to be distracted from our worries, and we quilt because it brings us joy. We quilt because we don't know what else to do, and we quilt because inspiration strikes.

We quilt for a thousand reasons and more, but why quilting? Surely there are common-interest communities surrounding almost any practice; what makes quilting unique?

Deep down I believe it has something to do with the tradition of the quilting bee, a group of people coming together to finish a quilt. I believe that the quilting bee is written into quilting in some fundamental ways; it speaks of quilting as a communal practice. It

It seems to me that community is the common thread that runs through the varied reasons why we quilt.

also carries with it an implicit invitation to come and be a part of something larger than oneself. The bee is part of the mythology of quilting, part of the fabric of the tradition. Though most quilts are made by individuals, in private, I believe there remains an elemental community at the heart of the practice itself.

It seems to me that community is the common thread that runs through the varied reasons why we quilt. Whether it is a literal participation in a guild or an online quilting group, or making quilts that speak about the communities we live in, that sense of community remains a constant within the quilting tradition. Precisely because quilting ties us to our fellow quilters, past and present, it prevents us from ever being entirely alone. And just maybe, therein lies the ultimate tug that quilting exerts: a reminder that our participation in the quilting tradition brings with it a more profound connectedness, a being with others whenever we pick up needle, thread, and cloth.

Smart Is Beautiful #1, Thomas Knauer, 2015, 79 × 79"
Each block in this quilt represents an alphabet letter using binary code; the position of the white square in each stripe determines the relationship of 0s and 1s. The quilt then as a whole spells out the words "smart is beautiful." I made this quilt as a reminder to my daughter that smart is indeed beautiful.

ACKNOWLEDGMENTS

I'd like to thank all of the quilters who contributed their work and words to this book. Your stories and stitches are essential to making this book whole.

I'd like to thank the whole team at Storey for bringing this book to life: Deborah for breathing life into the project from the beginning, Michal for finding a shape for my tumble of words, and Carolyn for taking it all and giving it form.

I'd like to thank all the bars and coffee shops that housed me for countless hours as I tapped away at my laptop.

I'd like to thank Katherine for all of her editing and suggestions. Without you I would likely have gone mad halfway through writing this book.

I'd like to thank all the quilt historians who pieced together the story of quilting. Your research has made the world a far richer place.

Finally, I'd like to thank the 1970s punk scene for existing and lending a soundtrack to the hours and hours (and hours) spent figuring this book out.

CONTRIBUTORS

Lynette Anderson
Little Quilt Store
www.littlequiltstore.com.au

Cheryl Brickey
Meadow Mist Designs
https://meadowmistdesigns.blogspot.com

Earamichia "Encyclopedia" Brown
www.cocktailsandthread.com

Alissa Haight Carlton
www.alissahaightcarlton.com

Jen Carlton Bailly
www.bettycrockerass.com

Joe Cunningham
www.joethequilter.com

Alexis Deise
www.alexisdeise.com

Malka Dubrawsky
A Stitch in Dye
www.stitchindye.com

Allison Dutton
Allison Sews
https://allison-sews.blogspot.com

Victoria Findlay Wolfe
Victoria Findlay Wolfe Quilts
vfwquilts.com

Jill Fisher
Pie Lady Quilts
https://pieladyquilts.blogspot.com

Marianne Fons
www.mariannefons.com

Mary Fons
www.maryfons.com

Amy Friend
During Quiet Time
https://duringquiettime.com

Amy Garro
13 Spools
www.13spools.com

Linda Gass
www.lindagass.com

Jacquie Gering
www.jacquiegering.com

Heather Givans
Crimson Tate
www.crimsontate.com

Hillary Goodwin
Entropy Always Wins
https://entropyalwayswinsblog.com

Jacey Gray
https://jaceycraft.blogspot.com

Debbie Grifka
Esch House Quilts
https://debbiegrifka.com

Laura Hartrich
www.laurahartrich.com

Brigitte Heitland
Zen Chic
www.brigitteheitland.de

Krista Hennebury
Poppyprint
https://poppyprintcreates.blogspot.com

Heather Jones
Heather Jones Studio
www.heatherjonesstudio.com

Nydia Kehnle
www.nydiakehnle.com

Chawne Kimber
https://cauchycomplete.wordpress.com

Jolene Klassen
Blue Elephant Stitches
https://blueelephantstitches.blogspot.com

Nicole Neblett
Mama Love Quilts
https://mamalovequilts.com

Stacey Lee O'Malley
https://slostudio.ca

Heidi Parkes
www.heidiparkes.com

Stephanie Zacharer Ruyle
Spontaneous Threads
spontaneousthreads.blogspot.com

Latifah Saafir
Latifah Saafir Studios
www.latifahsaafirstudios.com

Jennifer Sampou
www.jennifersampou.com

Denyse Schmidt
Denyse Schmidt Quilts
https://dsquilts.com

Molli Sparkles
https://mollisparkles.com

Anne Sullivan
Play Crafts
www.play-crafts.com/blog

Sherri Lynn Wood
www.sherrilynnwood.com

Casey York
www.casey-york.com

Kathy York
https://aquamoonartquilts.blogspot.com

INDEX OF HISTORICAL AND TECHNICAL TERMS

Field, Sherri Lynn Wood, 2016

ADDITIONAL PHOTOGRAPHY *continued*

International Quilt Study Center & Museum, University of Nebraska-Lincoln: 1997.007.0297, 39; 1997.007.0560, 41; 1997.007.0639, 77; 1997.007.0647, 42; 1997.007.0926E, 43; 2000.004.0002, 111; 2000.004.0009, 113; 2000.004.0059, 112; 2003.003.0089, 109; 2003.003.0104, 108; 2003.003.0355, 78; 2005.039.0001, 40; 2005.048.0007, 12; 2005.059.0001, 141, 142 (detail); 2006.003.0004, 10 b.; 2007.034.0001, 11; 2008.040.0001, 10 t.; 2008.040.0219, 9; 2011.003.0001, 79; © Jacquelyn D. Gering, 125, 127, 209 l.; Courtesy of Jen Carlton Bailly, 181; © Jenny Hallengren, 132; © Kathy York, 34, 146; © Latifah Saafir, v c.l., 172; © 2016 Linda Gass, 162 r., © 2017 Linda Gass, 162 l.; © 2005 Linda Gass, Photograph by Don Tuttle, 161; © 2012 Linda Gass, Photograph by Don Tuttle, 159, 163; © 2013 Linda Gass, Photograph by Don Tuttle, 156; © 2015 Linda Gass, Photograph by Don Tuttle, 75, 160; © 2018 Linda Gass, Photograph by Don Tuttle, 208 r.; © 2016 Linda Gass, Photograph by Jeff Rumans, 207; © Lynette Anderson, 66–70, 209 r.; Courtesy of Mary Fons, 93; Courtesy of Mitch Hopper, 16; © Molli Sparkles, 182–183; © Nydia Kehnle, 51; Octagon Shimmer Quilt by Jennifer Sampou, reprinted by permission of C&T Publishing, Inc. For further information visit jennifer-sampou.com or on Instagram @jennifersampou., v r., 4, 178; Quilt Museum and Gallery, York/© The Quilters' Guild of the British Isles/Bridgeman Images, 13 r.; © Sharon Risedorph, 62; © Sherri Lynn Wood, 190–195, 210; © Stacey Lee O'Malley, 102, 118; © Teddi Yaeger Photography, 188; © Thomas Knauer, vi, ix–x, 105, 205; © Victoria Findlay Wolfe, 96, 99; Courtesy of the Volckening Collection, 169; © Yvonne Fuchs, 155

from the studio of...

thomas knauer sews

title:

pieced by:

quilted by:

date:

Thomas Knauer began his career teaching design at Drake University before turning to quilting. He has designed fabrics for several leading manufacturers, and his work has been exhibited in quilt shows and museums across the globe, including the International Quilt Study Center & Museum, the New Museum of Contemporary Art, Des Moines Art Center, the Melbourne Fringe Festival, and the Cranbrook Art Museum. Knauer is the author of two previous books, including *The Quilt Design Coloring Workbook*. Find him online at www.thomasknauersews.com.

Modern art is the unlikely muse for quilting inspiration in this unique interactive guide. The 91 design prompts and full-page coloring templates help you try new color combinations and pattern experiments for your quilts.